INTRODUCTION

The short story was first recognized as a distinct class of literature in 1842, when Poe's criticism of Hawthorne[1] called attention to the new form of fiction. Short story writing had, however, been practiced for many years before that: perhaps the narratives of Homer and the tales of the first books of the Bible may be considered as the first examples; certainly the short story is closely associated in its early history with narrative poems, allegorical tales, and mouth-to-mouth traditions, and it can be traced surely to the *fabliaux* of the thirteenth century. Later writers aided in its development: Mallory's "Morte D'Arthur" and Caxton's popularization of old romances marked a further progress; and some of the work of Defoe and Addison would almost stand the modern tests. But the short story as we know it to-day is a product of the nineteenth century; and it owes its position in literature, if not its very existence, to the work of Irving, Hawthorne, and Poe. They first recognized its possibilities and employed it seriously; and the art and genius which they put into their tales assured the short story a permanent place in literature. They differed in subject matter and style, but they recognized the same requirements and limitations; and the canons which they established then obtain to-day.

The modern short story is essentially an American product; and our masters of its art have established precedents for literary workers of the old world. In England, Stevenson, Kipling and Haggard are considered the originators of the modern short story; and Zola, de Maupassant, Daudet and Paul Marguerite in France, Tolstoi in Russia, and other famous foreign authors have their claims for consideration; but all of them, admittedly or not, are but disciples of the earlier American trinity. This book will confine itself to the English-American short story.

To-day the short story is so popular that we seem to be in a new literary epoch—the epoch of the short story—and there is no apparent cause to expect an early diminution in the demand for such literature; so that to the young writer the short story offers the best opportunity to prove his mettle. Then, too, it has the additional value of being an excellent school for the novelist. The short story and the novel have many radical differences; but in material, treatment and aim they are much the same, and the same general training is necessary for both. All short story writers do not become great novelists, nor have all novelists been short story tellers; but it is a fact that the majority of the present day novelists served their 'prenticeship in the ranks of the short story writers.

FOOTNOTES:

[1] "Hawthorne's 'Tales,'" by Edgar Allan Poe. *Graham's Magazine*, May, 1842.

THE SHORT STORY

There is no modern literary form which is as little understood as is the short story. The term short story is applied to every piece of prose writing of 30,000 words or less, without regard to its matter, aim, or handling; but our purpose demands a definition of some accuracy.

"In the first place, then, what is, and what is *not*, a short story? Many things a short story may be. It may be an episode, like Miss Ella Hepworth Dixon's or like Miss Bertha Thomas'; a fairy tale, like Miss Evelyn Sharp's; the presentation of a single character with the stage to himself (Mr. George Gissing); a tale of the uncanny (Mr. Rudyard Kipling); a dialogue comedy (Mr. Pett Ridge); a panorama of selected landscape, a vision of the sordid street, a record of heroism, a remote tradition or some old belief vitalized by its bearing on our lives to-day, an analysis of an obscure calling, a glimpse at a forgotten quarter ... but one thing it can never be—it can never be 'a novel in a nutshell'."[2]

"A short story ... must lead up to something. It should have for its structure a plot, a bit of life, an incident such as you would find in a brief newspaper paragraph.... He (Richard Harding Davis) takes the substance of just such a paragraph, and, with that for the meat of his story, weaves around it details, descriptions and dialogue, until a complete story is the result. Now, a story is something more than incidents and descriptions. It is a definite thing. It progresses constantly. It arrives somewhere. It must enforce some idea (no matter what). It must be such a reality that a man who read it would carry away a definite impression."[3]

It is evident, then, that the term short story is properly used only when it means a short prose narrative, which presents artistically a bit of real life; the primary object of which is to amuse, though it may also depict a character, plead a cause, or point a moral; this amusement is neither of that æsthetic order which we derive from poetry, nor of that cheap sort which we gain from a broad burlesque: it is the simple yet intellectual pleasure derived from listening to a well told narrative.

The first requisite of a short story is that the writer have a story to tell—that is, a plot. He may present pretty scenes and word pictures if he will, but he must vivify and humanize them by the introduction of certain characters, patterned after the people of real life; and these characters must move and act and live. The presentation of "still life" pure and simple is not in the province of the short story.

The question of length is but relative; in general a short story should not exceed 10,000 words, and it could hardly contain less than 1,000; while from 3,000 to 5,000 is the most usual length. Yet Hawthorne's "The Gentle Boy" contains 12,000 words; Poe's "The Gold Bug," 13,000; and perhaps the majority of James' exceed the maximum, while "The Lesson of the Master" requires 25,000, and "The Aspern Papers" 32,000. Indeed, the length of any story is determined, not so much by some arbitrary word limit, as by the theme with which it deals. Every plot requires a certain number of words for its proper elaboration, and neither more nor less will do. Just what the limit for any particular story may be, the writer must decide for himself. "It seems to me that a short story writer should act, metaphorically, like this—he should put his idea for a story into one cup of a pair of balances, then into the other he should deal out his words; five hundred; a thousand; two thousand; three thousand; as the case may be—and when the number of words thus paid in causes the beam to rise, on which his idea hangs, then is his story finished. If he puts in a word more or less, he is doing false work."[4]

The short story does not need the love element that is generally considered necessary to the novel, and many short stories disregard it altogether. Love usually requires time and moods and varying scenes for its normal development, so that it is difficult to treat it properly within the limits of the short story; and then only when some particular phase or scene admits of isolation. Then, too, many short stories are merely accounts of strange adventures, wonderful discoveries or inventions, and queer occurrences of all sorts—themes which amuse us from their mere oddity; or they are verbal photographs of life, which are interesting from their views of psychological and sociological problems; and none of them requires love as the chief motive. Ingenuity and originality, the principal constituents of such tales, are the story teller's great virtues; on them he bases his hopes. Therefore, he must have strong individuality, and the power of forcing his readers to view life through his eyes, without perceiving him.

Also, and as if to compensate for the lack of the love interest, the short story has a "touch of fantasy" which gives it a distinctive charm. This quality is the hint of—not necessarily the supernatural, but rather the weird; it is a recognition and a vague presentation of the many strong influences that are not explainable by our philosophy of life. It is the intrusion into our matter-of-fact lives of the uncanny element, which the novice so grossly misuses in his tales of premonitory dreams and visions, and of most unghostly ghosts. "It is not enough to catch a ghost white-handed and to hale him into the full glare of the electric light. A brutal misuse of the supernatural is perhaps the very lowest degradation of the art of fiction. But 'to mingle the marvellous rather as a slight, delicate, and evanescent flavor than as any actual portion of the substance,' to quote from the preface to the 'House of the Seven Gables,' this is, or should be, the aim of the writer of short-stories whenever his feet leave the firm ground of fact as he strays in the unsubstantial realm of fantasy. In no one's writings is this better exemplified than in Hawthorne's; not even in Poe's. There is a propriety in

Hawthorne's fantasy to which Poe could not attain. Hawthorne's effects are moral where Poe's are merely physical. The situation and its logical development and the effects to be got out of it are all Poe thinks of. In Hawthorne the situation, however strange and weird, is only the outward and visible sign of an inward and spiritual struggle. Ethical consequences are always worrying Hawthorne's soul; but Poe did not know there were any ethics."[5]

The short story usually treats of the lighter and brighter side of life. It is seldom in deadly earnest; it tends somewhat to superficiality; and it prefers cleverness to profundity, in both conception and treatment. Naturally, then, comedy rather than tragedy is its usual sphere; and though the tale may end in gloom, it more frequently suggests a possible tragedy in order to heighten the effect of the happy denouement. For similar reasons the short story avoids the didactic tone, either presenting its lesson in clever disguise, or limiting its moral efforts to providing innocent amusement for an idle hour.

In the strife between realism and romanticism the short story adopts the middle course, taking advantage of the better phases of both, but siding with neither; for every life is subject to both influences, often at the same time, and the short story aspires to present life as it is. "Without true realism and genuine romanticism—actuality and ideals—good work was never done, nor did any writer ever rise to be an author."[6] "No worthy work of fiction may properly be labelled romantic, realistic or symbolic, since every great work of art contains all these in some proportion. Love and fighting are not necessarily romance; nor are soup-kitchens and divorce courts necessarily realism.... Malice, futility and ugliness—the dreadful monotony of existence—are not necessarily real life; nor the tales of summer love and marriage ceremonies, successful fightings, or sacrifice and chivalry necessarily romance."[7]

In its technique a short story demands the utmost care; it lacks the bulk of the novel, which hides minor defects. It must have a definite form, which shall be compact, and which shall have its parts properly proportioned and related; and it must be wrought out in a workmanlike manner. It requires extreme care from its conception to its completion, when it must stand forth a perfect work of art; and yet it must reveal no signs of the worker's tools, or of the pains by which it was achieved.

From what has been said it is evident that the short story is artificial, and to a considerable degree unnatural. It could hardly be otherwise, for it takes out of our complex lives a single person or a single incident and treats that as if it were complete in itself. Such isolation is not known to nature: There all things work together, and every man influences all about him and is influenced by them. Yet this separation and exclusion are required by the conventions of the short story; and after all, there is always the feeling, if the characters are well handled, that they have been living and will continue to live, though we have chanced to come in contact with them for only a short time.

It is this isolation, this magnifying of one character or incident, that constitutes the chief difference between the novel and the short story.[8] In the novel we have a reproduction of a certain period of real life: all the characters are there, with their complex lives and their varying emotions; there are varied scenes, each one the stage of some particular incident or semi-climax which carries the action on to the final chapter; and there are persons and scenes and conversations which have no reason for being there, except that just such trivial things are parts of life. With the short story it is very different: that permits of but one scene and incident, one or two real characters, with one predominant emotion: all else is a detriment to the interest and success of the story. A book may be called a novel even if it is composed of a series of incidents, each complete in itself, which are bound together by a slender thread of common characters; but a story cannot properly be called a short one unless it has simplicity of plot, singleness of character and climax, and freedom from extraneous matter. "In a short story the starting point is an idea, a definite notion, an incident, a surprising discovery; and this must have a definite significance, a bearing on our view of life; also it must be applied to the development of one life course, one character. The novel, on the other hand, starts with a conception of character, a man, a woman, a human heart, which under certain circumstances works out a definite result, makes a world.... Lastly it develops a group of characters, who together make a complete community, instead of tracing the life course of one."[9]

To prove that these various requirements are recognized and observed by masters of the art, I would ask you to consider the following list, which *The Critic* selected from nearly five hundred submitted in competition for a prize which it offered for a list of the best twelve American short stories:

"The Man Without a Country," Edward Everett Hale.

"The Luck of Roaring Camp," Bret Harte.

"The Great Stone Face," Nathaniel Hawthorne.

"The Snow Image," Nathaniel Hawthorne.

"The Gold Bug," Edgar Allan Poe.

"The Murders in the Rue Morgue," Edgar Allan Poe.

"The Lady, or the Tiger?" Frank R. Stockton.

"The Legend of Sleepy Hollow," Washington Irving.

"Rip Van Winkle," Washington Irving.

"Marse Chan," Thomas Nelson Page.

"Marjorie Daw," Thomas Bailey Aldrich.

"The Revolt of Mother," Mary E. Wilkins.[10]

FOOTNOTES:

[2] "The Short Story," by Frederick Wedmore. *Nineteenth Century*, Mar., '98.

[3] "How to Write Short Stories." An interview with F. Hopkinson Smith in the Boston *Herald. Current Literature*. June, '96.

[4] Robert Barr in "How to Write a Short Story; A Symposium." *The Bookman*. Mar., '97.

[5] "The Philosophy of the Short-story," by Brander Matthews. *Lippincott's*. Oct, '85.

[6] "Magazine Fiction and How Not to Write It," by Frederick M. Bird. *Lippincott's*. Nov., '94.

[7] "The Art of Fiction," by Gilbert Parker. *The Critic*, Dec.,'98.

[8] In many respects the art of the short story and the novel are so closely allied that I have been able to reenforce my observations with magazine articles which were meant to apply primarily to the novel.—THE AUTHOR.

[9] "How to Write Fiction." Published anonymously by Bellaires & Co., London. Part I, Chapter I.

[10] "The Best Twelve American Stories." *The Critic*. Apr. 10, '97.

SHORT STORIES CLASSIFIED

THE treatment demanded by any particular story depends more upon its class than upon the tale itself; a story which recounts an actual occurrence is much less exacting than one which attempts to depict manners; and, in general, the more the writer relies on his art, the more difficult is his task. It is therefore both possible and profitable to separate short stories into definite groups and to consider them collectively rather than as units. This classification is based chiefly upon the necessity of a plot, the purpose or aim of the narrative, and the skill and care required for its successful treatment. It is crude and arbitrary from a literary standpoint, for a good short story is capable of being listed under several different classes, but it serves our practical purpose. Each story is placed according to its dominant class; and the classes are arranged progressively from the simplest to the most difficult of treatment. The examples are presented only as definite illustrations; there is no attempt to classify all short stories, or all the stories of any particular author.

I. THE TALE is the relation, in an interesting and literary form, of some simple incident or stirring fact. It has no plot in the sense that there is any problem to unravel, or any change in the relation of the characters; it usually contains action, but chiefly accidents or odd happenings, which depend on their intrinsic interest, without regard to their influence on the lives of the actors.

(*a*) It is often a genuine *True Story*, jealously observant of facts, and embellished only to the extent that the author has endeavored to make his style vivid and picturesque. Such stories are a result of the tendency of the modern newspaper to present its news in good literary form. The best illustrations are the occasional contributions of Ray Stannard Baker to *McClure's Magazine*.

(*b*) It may, however, be an *Imaginative Tale*, which could easily happen, but which is the work of the author's imagination. It is a straightforward narration of possible events; if it passes the bounds of probability, or attempts the utterly impossible, it becomes a *Story of Ingenuity*.(See Class VIII.) It has no love element and no plot; and its workmanship is loose. The best examples are the stories of adventure found in the better class of boys' and children's papers.

II. THE MORAL STORY, in spite of the beautiful examples left us by Hawthorne, is usually too baldly didactic to attain or hold a high place in literature. Its avowed purpose is to preach, and, as ordinarily written, preach it does in the most determined way. Its plot is usually just sufficient to introduce the moral. It is susceptible of a high literary polish in the hands of a master; but when attempted by a novice it is apt to degenerate into a mess of moral platitudes.

(*a*) *The Fable* makes no attempt to disguise its didactic purpose, but publishes it by a final labelled "Moral," which epitomizes the lesson it conveys. In *Fables* the characters are often animals, endowed with all the attributes of men. It early lost favor because of its bald didacticism, and for the last century has been practiced only occasionally. To-day it is used chiefly for the purpose of burlesque and satire, as in George Ade's "Fables in Slang." Æsop is of course the immortal example of this sort of story.

(*b*) The *Story with a Moral* attempts to sugar-coat its sermon with a little narrative. It sticks rather closely to facts, and has a slight plot, which shows, or is made to show, the consequences of drinking, stealing, or some other sin. Usually it is either brutally realistic or absurdly exaggerated; but that it can be given literary charm is proved by Hawthorne's use of it. Maria Edgeworth is easily the "awful example" of this class, and her stories, such as "Murad the Unlucky" and "The Grateful Negro," are excellent illustrations of how *not* to write. Many of Hawthorne's tales come under this head, especially "Lady Eleanor's Mantle," "The Ambitious Guest," and "Miss Bullfrog." The stories of Miss Wilkins usually have a strong moral element, but they are better classed in a later division. (See Class IV.) Contemporary examples of this style of writing may be found in the pages of most Sunday School and Temperance papers.

(*c*) *The Allegory* is the only really literary form of the *Moral Story*, and the only one which survives to-day. It has a strong moral purpose, but disguises it under the pretense of a well-told story; so that it is read for its story alone, and the reader is conscious of its lesson only when he has finished the narrative. It usually personifies or gives concrete form to the various virtues and vices of men. Examples: Hawthorne's "The Birthmark," "Rappaccini's Daughter," and "Feathertop." Allegories which deserve the name are sometimes found in current periodicals.

III. THE WEIRD STORY owes its interest to the innate love of the supernatural or unexplainable which is a part of our complex human nature—the same feeling which prompts a group of children to beg for "just one more" ghost story, while they are still shaken with the terror of the last one. It may have a definite plot in which supernatural beings are actors; but more often it is slight in plot, but contains a careful psychological study of some of the less pleasant emotions.

(*a*) The *Ghost Story* usually has a definite plot, in which the ghost is an actor. The ghost may be a "really truly" apparition, manifesting itself by the conventional methods, and remaining unexplained to the end, as in Irving's "The Spectre Bridegroom," and Kipling's "The Phantom 'Rickshaw;" or it may prove to be the result of a superstitious mind dwelling upon perfectly natural occurrences, as in Irving's "The Legend of Sleepy Hollow," and Wilkins' "A Gentle Ghost." It requires art chiefly to render it plausible; particularly in the latter case, when the mystery must be carefully kept up until the denouement.

(*b*) The *Fantastic Tale* treats of the lighter phases of the supernatural. Its style might be well described as whimsical, its purpose is to amuse by means of playful fancies, and it usually exhibits a delicate humor. The plot is slight and subordinate. Examples: Hawthorne's "A Select Party," "The Hall of Fantasy," and "Monsieur du Miroir;" and most of our modern fairy tales.

(*c*) The *Study in Horror* was first made popular by Poe, and he has had almost no successful imitators. It is unhealthy and morbid, full of a terrible charm if well done, but tawdry and disgusting if bungled. It requires a daring imagination, a full and facile vocabulary, and a keen sense of the ludicrous to hold these two in check. The plot is used only to give the setting to the story. Most any of Poe's tales would serve as an illustration, but "The Pit and the Pendulum," and "The Fall of the House of Usher" are particularly apt. Doyle has done some work approaching Poe's, but his are better classed as *Stories of Ingenuity*. ([See Class VIII](.).)

IV. THE CHARACTER STUDY is a short story in which the chief interest rests in the development and exposition of human character. It may treat of either a type or an individual. Good character delineation is one of the surest proofs of a writer's literary ability.

(*a*) When the character depicted is inactive the resultant work is not really a story. It usually has no plot, and is properly a *Sketch*, in which the author makes a psychological analysis of his subject. It inclines to superficiality and is liable to degenerate into a mere detailed description of the person. It demands of the writer the ability to catch striking details and to present them vividly and interestingly. Examples: Hawthorne's "Sylph Etherege" and "Old Esther Dudley;" Poe's "The Man of the Crowd;" James' "Greville Fane" and "Sir Edmund Orme;" Stevenson's "Will o' the Mill;" Wilkins' "The Scent of the Roses" and "A Village Lear."

(*b*) When the character described is active we have a *Character Study* proper, built upon a plot which gives the character opportunity to work out his own personality before us by means of speech and action. The plot is subordinated to the character sketching. The psychological analysis is not presented by the author in so many words, but is deduced by the reader from his observation of the character. Such studies constitute one of the highest art forms of the short story, for the characters must live on the printed page. The short stories of Henry James and of Miss Wilkins could almost be classed *in toto* under this head; Miss Wilkins' characters are usually types, while those of James are more often individual, though rather unusual. Other good examples are Hawthorne's "Edward Randolph's Portrait;" Irving's "The Devil and Tom Walker," and "Wolfert Weber;" Stevenson's "Markheim" and "The Brown Box;" and Davis' "Van Bibber," as depicted in the several stories of "Van Bibber and Others."

Notice that in both subdivisions nearly every title embodies a reference to the character described, showing that the author intentionally set out to sketch a character.

V. THE DIALECT STORY might be considered as a subdivision of the preceding class, since it is in effect a *Character Study*; but its recent popularity seems to warrant its being treated separately. Its chief distinction is that it is written in the broken English used by the uneducated classes of our own country, and by foreigners. Its plot is either very slight or hopelessly hackneyed, and it is redeemed from sheer commonplace only by its picturesque language. It is usually told in the first person by some English-murdering ignoramus. It is simple, and sometimes has a homely pathos. It may present character as either active or inactive, though usually the former. Its excuse for existence is that it gives truthful expression, in their own language, to the thoughts of certain classes of society; but as written by the amateur the dialect is a fearful and wonderful combination of incorrect English that was never heard from the mouth of any living man. Joel Chandler Harris' "Nights with Uncle Remus" contains genuine dialect; other varieties correctly handled may be found in almost any of the stories of George Washington Cable, Ian Maclaren, and Miss Wilkins.

The *Dialect Story* as literature and as a field for the novice is considered at length in Chapter VI.

VI. THE PARABLE OF THE TIMES is a short story which aims to present a vivid picture of our own times, either to criticise some existing evil, or to entertain by telling us something of how "the other half" of the world lives. It is in a sense a further development of *The Tale* (Class I.), though it has a more definite plot. It is the most favored form of the short story to-day, and its popularity is responsible for a mess of inane commonplace and bald realism that is written by amateurs, who think they are presenting pen pictures of life. For since its matter is gathered from our everyday lives, it requires some degree of skill to make such narratives individual and interesting.

(*a*) The *Instructive Story* of this class may be further subdivided as (1) that which puts present day problems in concrete form, with no attempt at a solution; and (2) that which not only criticises, but attempts also to correct. In either case, it aims to reform by education; it deals with actual problems of humanity rather than with abstract moral truths; and it seeks to amuse always, and to reform if possible. It must not be confused with the *Moral Story* of Class II. Octave Thanet writes this style of story almost exclusively, and any of her work selected at random would be a good illustration; her "Sketches of American Types" would be listed under (1), and such stories as "The Scab" and "Trusty No. 49" under (2). Under (1) would come also Brander Matthews' "Vignettes of Manhattan;" and under (2) Edward Everett Hale's "The Man Without a Country" and "Children of the Public."

(*b*) The most usual story of this class is the *Story of To-day*, which uses present day conditions as a background, and which endeavors only to amuse and interest the reader. Naturally, however, since the scenes and persons described must be new to the reader, such a story is also educating and broadening in its influence. Its plot may seem trivial when analyzed, but it is selected with a view more to naturalness than to strength or complexity. Here we should list nearly all of our modern so-called "society stories," and "stories of manners." Any of Richard Harding Davis' short stories will serve as an excellent illustration, and most of the stories in current periodicals belong in the same category.

VII. THE STORY OF INGENUITY is one of the most modern forms of the short story, and, if I may be pardoned the prolixity, one of the most ingenious. It might be called the "fairy tale of the grown-up," for its interest depends entirely upon its appeal to the love for the marvelous which no human being ever outgrows. It requires fertility of invention, vividness of imagination, and a plausible and convincing style. Yet it is an easy sort of story to do successfully, since ingenuity will atone for many technical faults; but it usually lacks serious interest and is short lived. Poe was the originator and great exemplar of the *Story of Ingenuity*, and all of his tales possess this cleverness in some degree.

(*a*) The *Story of Wonder* has little plot. It is generally the vivid description of some amazing discovery (Poe's "Some Words with a Mummy," Hale's "The Spider's Eye"), impossible invention (Adee's "The Life Magnet," Mitchell's "The Ablest Man in the World"), astounding adventure (Stockton's "Wreck of the Thomas Hyde," Stevenson's "House with Green Blinds"), or a vivid description of what might be (Benjamin's "The End of New

York," Poe's "The Domain of Arnheim"). It demands unusual imaginative power.

(*b*) The *Detective Story* requires the most complex plot of any type of short story, for its interest depends solely upon the solution of the mystery presented in that plot. It arouses in the human mind much the same interest as an algebraic problem, which it greatly resembles. Poe wrote the first, and probably the best, one in "The Murders in the Rue Morgue;" his "The Mystery of Marie Roget" and "The Gold Bug" are other excellent examples. Doyle, in his "Sherlock Holmes" stories, is a worthy successor of Poe.

VIII. THE HUMOROUS STORY almost belongs in the category of *Stories of Ingenuity*, so largely does it depend upon the element of the unusual; but for that fact it should have been listed earlier, because it has little care for plot. Indeed, these stories are the freest of all in their disregard for conventions; with them it is "anything to raise a laugh," and the end is supposed to justify the means. In general they are of transient interest and crude workmanship, little fitted to be called classics; but Mark Twain, at least, has shown us that humor and art are not incompatible.

(*a*) The simplest form is the *Nonsense Story*, as it may be justly called. Usually it has the merest thread of plot, but contains odd or grotesque characters whose witty conversation furnishes all the amusement necessary. If the characters do act they have an unfortunate tendency to indulge in horse play. The work of John Kendrick Bangs well illustrates this type of story. His books, "The House Boat on the Styx" and "The Pursuit of the House Boat," are really only collections of short stories, for each chapter can be considered as a whole.

(*b*) *The Burlesque* has a plot, but usually one which is absurdly impossible, or which is treated in a burlesque style. The amusement is derived chiefly from the contrast between the matter and the method of its presentation. Most of Stockton's stories are of this type: notably his "The Lady, or the Tiger?" Mark Twain, too, usually writes in this vein, as in "The Jumping Frog" and "The Stolen White Elephant."

IX. THE DRAMATIC STORY is the highest type of the short story. It requires a definite but simple plot, which enables the characters to act out their parts. In its perfect form it is the "bit of real life" which it is the aim of the short story to present. It is the story shorn of all needless verbiage, and told as nearly as possible in the words and actions of the characters themselves; and it possesses a strong climax. Therefore it demands the most careful and skillful workmanship, from its conception to its final polishing. It is the most modern type of the short story.

(*a*) The short story has *Dramatic Form* when the author's necessary comments correspond to the stage directions of the drama. Such a story is, in fact, a miniature drama, and is often capable of being acted just as it stands. It has a definite plot, but it is developed by dialogue as frequently as by action. It is the extreme of the modern tendency toward dramatic narrative, and is just a little too "stagey" and artificial to be a perfect short story. It is, however, in good literary standing and in good favor with the public, and it is most excellent practice for the tyro, for in it he has to sink himself completely in his characters. Examples: Hope's "The Dolly Dialogues;" Kipling's "The Story of the Gadsbys;" and Howells' one act parlor plays, like "The Parlor Car," "The Register," "The Letter," and "Unexpected Guests."

(*b*) A short story has *Dramatic Effect* when it deals with a single crisis, conveys a single impression, is presented chiefly by the actors themselves, and culminates in a single, perfect climax. It may, or may not, be capable of easy dramatization. It is less artificial than the story of pure *Dramatic Form*, but is just as free from padding and irrelevant matter, and just as vivid in effect. It allows of greater art and finish, for the writer has wider freedom in his method of presentation. Examples: Poe's "'Thou Art the

Man!'" and "Berenice;" James' "The Lesson of the Master" and "A Passionate Pilgrim;" Wilkins' "A New England Nun" and "Amanda and Love;" Stevenson's "The Isle of the Voices;" and Irving's "The Widow and Her Son" and "Rip Van Winkle." But, indeed, every good short story belongs in this class, which is not so much a certain type of the short story, as the "honor class" to which each story seeks admittance.

Every story cited in this book, unless otherwise located, can be found in one of the appended published collections of short stories:

George Ade: "Fables in Slang."

John Kendrick Bangs: "The Bicyclers;" "Ghosts I Have Met;" "The Houseboat on the Styx;" "Mantel-Piece Minstrels, and Other Stories;" "Paste Jewels;" "The Pursuit of the Houseboat;" "The Water-Ghost and Others."

J. M. Barrie: "An Auld Licht Manse;" "Auld Licht Idyls."

George Washington Cable: "Old Creole Days;" "Strange True Stories of Louisiana."

Samuel L. Clemens (Mark Twain): "Merry Tales;" "The Stolen White Elephant."

Richard Harding Davis: "Cinderella and Others;" "The Exiles and Other Stories;" "Gallegher, and Other Stories;" "The Lion and the Unicorn;" "Van Bibber and Others."

Charles Dickens: "Christmas Books;" "Christmas Stories;" "Sketches by Boz."

A. Conan Doyle: "The Adventures of Sherlock Holmes;" "The Captain of the Pole Star;" "The Exploits of Brigadier Gerard;" "Memoirs of Sherlock Holmes;" "My Friend the Murderer;" "Round the Red Lamp."

Maria Edgeworth: "Popular Tales."

Alice French (Octave Thanet): "A Book of True Lovers;" "The Missionary Sheriff;" "Stories of a Western Town."

H. Rider Haggard: "Allan's Wife."

Joel Chandler Harris: "Daddy Jake, the Runaway;" "Nights with Uncle Remus;" "Tales of Home Folks in Peace and War."

Bret Harte: "Colonel Starbottle's Client;" "In the Hollow of the Hills;" "The Luck of Roaring Camp;" "Mrs. Skagg's Husbands;" "Tales of the Argonauts;" "Thankful Blossom;" "The Story of a Mine."

Nathaniel Hawthorne: "Mosses from an Old Manse;" "Twice Told Tales."

Anthony Hope: "The Dolly Dialogues."

William Dean Howells: "A Fearful Responsibility and Other Stories;" "The Mouse-Trap and Other Farces;" "The Sleeping Car and Other Farces."

Washington Irving: "The Sketch Book;" "Tales of a Traveler."

Henry James: "The Aspern Papers;" "The Author of Beltraffio;" "The Lesson of the Master;" "A London Life;" "A Passionate Pilgrim;" "The Real Thing."

Rudyard Kipling: "The Day's Work;" "In Black and White;" "Indian Tales;" "The Jungle Book;" "Life's Handicap;" "Many Inventions;" "The Phantom 'Rickshaw;" "Plain Tales from the Hills;" "The Second Jungle Book;" "Soldiers Three and Military Tales;" "Soldier Stories;" "Under the Deodars."

Brander Matthews: "Outlines in Local Color;" "Tales of Fantasy and Fact;" "Vignettes of Manhattan."

Guy de Maupassant: "The Odd Number."

Thomas Nelson Page: "The Burial of the Guns;" "In Ole Virginia."

Scribner's series: "Short Stories by American Authors."

Robert Louis Stevenson: "The Island Nights' Entertainments;" "The Merry Men;" "New Arabian Nights."

Frank R. Stockton: "Amos Kilbright;" "The Lady, or the Tiger?" "Rudder Grange;" "A Story Teller's Pack."

John Watson (Ian Maclaren): "Auld Lang Syne;" "Beside the Bonnie Brier Bush."

Mary E. Wilkins: "A Humble Romance;" "The Love of Parson Lord;" "A New England Nun;" "The Pot of Gold;" "Silence;" "Young Lucretia."

III

THE PLOT

THE plot is the nucleus of the story, the bare thought or incident upon which the narrative is to be builded. When a child says, "Grandma, tell me the story of how the whale swallowed Jonah," he gives the plot of the story that he desires; and the grandmother proceeds to elaborate that primal idea to suit the taste of her auditor. In like manner, before you put pen to paper, you must have in mind some interesting idea which you wish to express in narrative form; the absence of such an idea means that you have no plot, no story to tell, and therefore have no business to be writing. If you undertake to tell a short story, go about it in a workmanlike manner: don't begin scribbling pretty phrases, and trust to Providence to introduce the proper story, but yourself provide the basic facts. If you do not begin correctly, it is useless for you to begin at all.

A plot implies action—that is, something must happen; at the conclusion of the story the characters must be differently situated, and usually differently related one to another, from what they were at the beginning. The event need not be tragic, or even serious; but it must be of sufficient importance, novelty and interest to justify its relation in narrative form. In general the plot of a short story involves an incident or a minor crisis in a human life, rather than the supreme crisis which makes or mars a man for good. The chief reason for this is that the supreme crisis requires more elaborate preparation and treatment than is possible in the short story. There may be a strong tragic element which makes it seem that the denouement must be tragic, but that is usually to obtain the effect of contrast. Yet the short story may be a supreme crisis and a tragedy, as are Stevenson's "Markheim," Hawthorne's "The Ambitious Guest"[11] and "The Birthmark," and many of Poe's tales; but these are stories of an exceptional type, in which the whole life of the chief actor comes to a focus in the crisis which makes the story.

The short story plot must be simple and complete. The popular idea of a plot, derived from the requirements of the novel and the drama, is that it should be a tangled skein of facts and fancies, which the author shall further complicate in order to exhibit his deftness in the final disentanglement. Such a plot is impossible for the short story, which admits of no side issues and no second or under plot. It must not be the synopsis of a novel, or the attempt to compress into the tiny compass of the short story a complicated plot sufficient for a novel, as are so many of the "Short Stories of the Day" now published by newspapers. As nearly as possible it must deal with a single person, in a single action, at a single place, in a single time. More than any other modern form of literature, the short story requires the observance of the old Greek unities of time, place and action: its brevity and compactness do not admit of the proper treatment of the changes wrought by the passage of time, the influences of different scenes, or the complications resulting from the interrelation of many characters of varied importance. If the plot chosen requires the passage of ten years' time, if it involves a shift of scene from New York to Timbuctoo, or if it introduces two or three sets of characters, it may by some miracle of ingenuity make a readable story, but it will never be a model one. In "The Ambitious Guest" the time is less than three hours, the place is a single room, and the action is the development of the guest's ambition.

Yet the plot is only relatively important. It must always be present or there is no story; but once there it takes second place. The short story is not written to exploit the plot, however clever that may be, but to give a glimpse of real life; and the plot is only a means to that end. This is well illustrated by the *Character Study*, in which the real interest centers in the analysis and exposition of a character, and the plot is incidental. In many classes of stories, as we have already observed, the plot is used only to hold the narrative together, and the interest depends on the attractiveness of the picture presented. The plot must not be allowed to force itself through the fabric of the story, like the protruding ribs of a half-starved horse; but must be made to give form and substantiality to the word-flesh which covers it.

In *Detective Stories*, however, the plot is all-important, for the interest depends entirely upon the unraveling of some tangle; but even here it must contain but a single idea, though that may be rather involved. Such stories are really much simpler than they appear, for their seeming complexity consists in telling the story backwards, and so reasoning from effect to cause, rather than vice versa as in the ordinary tale. The plot itself is simple enough, as may be proved by working backward through Poe's "The Murders in the Rue Morgue." This is, by the way, a method of plot-making which is often, and incorrectly, employed by novices in the construction of any story. It has been aptly called "building the pyramid from the apex downward."[12] It results from an exaggerated conception of the importance of the plot. But it is not so much *what* the characters do that interests us, but *how* they do it.

"The true method for the making of a plot is the development of what may be called a plot-germ. Take two or three characters, strongly individualized morally and mentally, place them in a strong situation and let them develop.... There are hundreds of these plot-germs in our every-day life, conversation and newspaper reading, and the slightest change in the character at starting will give a wide difference in ending.... Change the country and the atmosphere is changed, the elements are subjected to new influences which develop new incidents and so a new plot.... Change any vital part in any character and the plot must be different. One might almost say two plots thus developed from the same plot-germ can have no greater resemblance than two shells cast up by the ocean."[13] "In the evolution of a plot the main things to be considered are that it shall be reasonably interesting, that it shall not violate probability, and that it shall possess some originality either of subject or of treatment. Not the possible, but the probable, should be the novelist's guide."[14]

The surest test of a usable plot is, "Is it natural?" Every plot is founded upon fact, which may be utilized in its original form, or so skillfully disguised or ingeniously distorted that it will seem like a product of the imagination. In the first case the resulting story would be termed realistic, in the second case romantic. A story built on a plot that is an unvarnished fact will be of course a *True Story*; and there are incidents and events in real life that need little more than isolation to make them good stories. There is, however, a danger that the novice may consider any matter usable which is true to life. Do not forget that the short story is a form of art.[15]

The best plot is derived from the action of an artistic imagination on a commonplace fact; the simpler and better known the fact is, the better will it serve the purpose, for it must be accepted without question: then it must be built up and developed by imaginative touches, always with a view to plausibility, till it attains the dignity of a distinct and interesting plot. Recent discoveries and the attainments of modern science have introduced us to so many strange things that we have almost ceased to doubt any statement which we may see in print; and writers have become so ingenious in weaving together fact and fancy that their tales are sometimes more plausible than truth itself. This was done with peculiar skill by Poe. His story, now known as "The Balloon Hoax," originally appeared in the New York *Sun* as a correspondent's account of an actual occurrence. The tale gained credence through its remarkable accuracy of detail in regard to recognized scientific principles, and the fact that at that time the world was considerably agitated by similar genuine feats of aerostation. As Poe makes one of his characters to say, "the feat is only so feasible that the sole wonder is why men have scrupled to attempt it before"—at least on paper.

Yet in spite of the many curious and interesting things that happen daily, and in spite of the inventive faculty of the mind, it is impossible to find a new plot. "History repeats itself" in small affairs as well as in great, and the human mind has not changed materially since the first days of story telling. Indeed, some one has said that all the stories ever told can be traced to less than a dozen original plots, whose origin is lost in obscurity. But if we can neither find nor invent a new story we can at least ring the changes on the old ones, and in this lies our hope to-day. Each one of these old plots is capable of an infinite variety of phases, and what we are constantly hailing as an original story is merely one of our old friends looked at from a different point of view. How many good, fresh stories have you read that were based on the ancient elemental plot of two men in love with one woman, or on that equally hoary one of fond lovers severed by disapproving parents? Irving's "The Legend of Sleepy Hollow" is derived from the first, yet few readers would so recognize it on first perusal; for unless you stop and analyze it, it seems distinct and new.

For further illustration of this reworking of old ideas, I have carefully searched the leading American magazines for March, 1900, for short stories based upon the old, old elemental plot of two men in love with one woman, and append herewith rough synopses of such stories. Note that this one number of *The Munsey* contains no less than three stories with this basic plot.

The Munsey.

"The Folly of It," by Ina Brevoort.

Fred Leighton and John Marchmont are in love with Angela. She loves Leighton, but they have agreed that he is too poor to make their married life happy. Marchmont, who is rich, proposes to her. She and Leighton calmly discuss the situation at their last dinner together and confirm their former decision; but when the matter is logically settled they decide to defy poverty and marry.

"With a Second to Spare," by Tom Hall.

Labarre and I both love Nellie, but Nellie marries me. Labarre leads a big strike on the railroad by which we are both employed as engineers; I refuse to join. One noon Labarre overpowers me, binds me on the rails between the wheels of my engine, and starts it moving slowly so that it will crush me by twelve, when Nellie always brings my dinner. After my death he expects to marry her. Nellie arrives and releases me just in the nick of time. (This story is really a scene from an amateur melodrama.)

"Mulligan's Treachery," by David H. Talmadge.

Mulligan and Garvey love Ellen Kelly. They agree not to take advantage of each other in wooing her, and go to the Philippines together as soldiers. There Garvey, leading a charge, is shot through the head, but Mulligan goes on and receives a medal for his bravery. Garvey recovers, but is blind for life. On their return to America Mulligan finds Ellen's face terribly mutilated by an accident. He would still gladly marry her; but he makes Garvey believe he won the medal, tells him nothing of Ellen's disfigurement, and brings about their marriage. Then he is conscience stricken at the manner in which he has taken advantage of his friend's disability.

The Cosmopolitan.

"The Pilot of the 'Sadie Simmons,'" by Joseph Mills Hanson.

Tommy Duncan, a Mississippi River pilot, is engaged to Tillie Vail. Her affections are alienated by Jack Cragg, a disreputable steamboat engineer, whom Duncan, believing he is deceiving the girl, threatens to kill on sight. Cragg kills a man in a drunken brawl on shore, and Duncan assists the sheriff to save him from would-be lynchers, and swears to protect him, before he knows who the prisoner is. When he learns he refuses to be bound by his oath, but as he is about to carry out his threat he is led to believe that Cragg honestly loves the girl. Cragg is attacked by a mob, and, though he cannot swim, jumps into the river to escape. Duncan rescues him and loses his own life. Cragg reforms and marries Tilly.

Ainslee's Magazine.

"Mr. Sixty's Mistake," by Chauncey C. Hotchkiss.

William Lewis loves Lillian Blythe. His brother Tom comes between them and William shoots him and flees west to Pleasant Valley, where he goes by the name of "Cockey Smith". One night he tells his story to his companions. Harry Blythe, brother to Lillian, Lewis' old friend, and now sheriff of his home county, who arrived that night, overhears him. Blythe reveals his identity to "Sixty", the butt of the camp, and tells him that Tom did not die and that Lewis can go back home, where Lillian is still waiting for him. Sixty breaks the news to Lewis while the latter is mad with drink, and Lewis, thinking the sheriff has come for him, kills him. Later he shoots himself.

"A Kentucky Welcome," by Ewan Macpherson.

Edmund Pierce, a New Yorker, is in love with Lucy Cabell, a Kentucky belle; and hearing that her cousin, "Brook" Cabell, is endangering his chances, he sets out to pay Miss Cabell a visit. He gets off at the wrong station and in his confusion is arrested by the local marshal as a Russian diamond robber. He telegraphs to the Cabells, and Brook rescues him at the point of the revolver, though he knows that the Northerner is Miss Cabell's favorite.

These stories, even in this crude, condensed form, robbed of all the beauties of imagery and expression, reveal the virtues which won for them editorial approval and which contribute to the enjoyment of their readers. Their apparent freshness is due to the treatment of a thread-bare plot in a new phase, and the phase, in turn, depends upon the introduction of some new element, unimportant in itself, perhaps, which presents the old story in the new light. "The Folly of It" is the best illustration, for though its plot is old and apparently hopeless, the brightness and naturalness of the conversation which constitutes almost the entire story makes it most readable. In "Mulligan's Treachery" the personality of Mulligan gives the necessary freshness. "The Pilot of the 'Sadie Simmons'" depends on local color and the interest in Duncan's struggle to distinguish right from wrong. And so some little freshness of treatment makes each of the others a good story.

These vivifying elements are by no means extraordinary, or difficult to find. They are new ideas concerning old subjects, such as you are continually meeting in your everyday life and reading. A new character, a new scene, a new invention or discovery, or merely a new mental bias on the part of the writer, will work wonders in the revivifying of an old plot. Think how many new phases of old plots have been produced recently by the incorporation of the "X" ray, or by the influence of the war with Spain. Try, then, to get a new light on the plot that you purpose to use, to view it from an unexpected side, to handle it in an unusual manner—in short, try to be original. If you have not the energy or the ability to do this, you would better cease your literary efforts at once, for you will only waste your time.

"But ... there are some themes so hackneyed—such as the lost will, the glorified governess, or the persecuted maiden who turns out to be an earl's daughter—that they would not now be tolerated outside the pages of a 'penny dreadful,' where, along with haughty duchesses, elfin-locked gypsies and murderous abductors, they have become part of the regular stock-in-trade of the purveyors of back-stairs literature. The only theme that never grows trite or commonplace is love."[16] "Another offense ... is the light theme that, being analyzed, amounts to nothing. It may be so cleverly handled that we read with pleasure—and then at the end are disgusted with ourselves for being pleased, and enraged at the writer for deluding us; for we thought there would be something beneath his graceful manners and airy persiflage, and lo, there is not."[17]

The plot of a short story should allow of expression in a single short, fairly simple sentence; if it cannot be so compressed there is something radically wrong with it. This may be called the "elemental" or "true" plot. It will be in general, perhaps vague, terms, and will permit differing treatment by different writers; yet its trend and its outcome will be definitely fixed. This true plot, in turn, can be expressed in yet more general terms, often as the primal truth which the story illustrates; this may be called the "theme" of the story. Thus in "The Ambitious Guest," the theme is "The futility of abstracted ambition;" or, in its most general terms, "The irony of fate." The true plot is:

An unknown but ambitious youth stops at a mountain tavern and perishes with its inmates.

In the development of a plot from this germ into the completed story, it is often of advantage to make what may be called a "skeleton" or "working plot." This skeleton is produced by thinking through the story as it has been conceived, and setting down on paper in logical order a line for every important idea. These lines will roughly correspond to the paragraphs of the finished story, but in a descriptive paragraph one line will not suffice, while a line may represent a dozen paragraphs of dialogue; then, too, paragraphing is partly logical and partly mechanical, and varies considerably with the person.

Working Plot of "The Ambitious Guest."

¶ 1.

The scene is a tavern located at the Notch in the White Hills.

The time, a September night.

The place is in danger from landslides and falling stones.

The family—father, mother, grandmother, daughter and children—are gathered happily about the hearth.

¶ 2, 3.

The tavern is on a well-frequented road.

¶ 4-7.

A young stranger enters, looking rather travel-worn, but quickly brightens up at his warm reception.

¶ 8, 9.

A stone rolls down the mountain side.

¶ 10.

The guest, though naturally reticent, soon becomes familiar with the family.

¶ 11.

The secret of the young man's character is high and abstracted ambition.

¶ 12.

He is as yet unknown.

¶ 13, 14.

He is sensible of the ludicrous side of his ambition.

¶ 15.

The daughter is not ambitious.

¶ 16-19.

The father's ambition is to own a good farm, to be sent to General Court, and to die peacefully.

¶ 20-23.

The children wish for the most ridiculous things.

¶ 24-27.

A wagon stops before the inn, but drives on when the landlord does not immediately appear.

¶ 28-31.

The daughter is not really content.

¶ 32.

The family picture.

¶ 33-37.

The grandmother tells of having prepared her grave-clothes.

Fears if they are not put on smoothly she will not rest easily.

¶ 38, 39.

She wishes to see herself in her coffin.

¶ 40, 41.

They hear the landslide coming.

¶ 42.

All rush from the house and are instantly destroyed.

The house is unharmed.

The bodies are never found.

¶ 43, 44.

Even the death of the ambitious guest is in doubt.

You will notice that this working plot omits many little details which are too trivial to set down, or which probably would not occur to one until the actual writing; and all the artistic touches that make the story literature are ruthlessly shorn away, for they are part of the treatment, not of the plot.

This method of permitting you to study your crude material in the concrete will prove of value to you. It enables you to crystalize into ideas what were mere phantasms of the brain, to arrange your thoughts in their proper order, and to condense or expand details with a ready comprehension of the effect of such alterations upon the general proportions of the story. It makes your purposed work objective enough so that you can consider it with a coolness and impartiality which were impossible while it was still in embryo in your brain; and it often reveals the absurdity or impossibility of a plan which had seemed to you most happy. I believe that the novice can do no better than to put his every story to this practical test.

The use of this skeleton in the further development of the story depends upon the methods of the writer, or the matter in hand. Many short story writers waste no time in preparations, but at once set down the story complete; and to my mind that is the ideal method, for it is more apt to make the tale spontaneous and technically correct. But if the story is not well defined in your mind, or if it requires some complexity of plot, like the *Detective Story*, this plan can be followed to advantage in the completion of the work. It may be used as a regular skeleton, upon which the narrative is built by a process of elaboration and expansion of the lines into paragraphs; or it may be used merely as a reference to keep in mind the logical order of events. Usually you will forget the scheme in the absorption of composition; but the fact of having properly arranged your ideas will assist you materially, if unconsciously, in the elaboration.

FOOTNOTES:

[11] "The Ambitious Guest," because of its technical perfection and its apt illustration of the principles discussed, will be used throughout as a paradigm. It can be found in full in the Appendix.—THE AUTHOR.

[12] "Have the Plots Been Exhausted?" Editorial Comment. *Current Literature.* June, '96.

[13] "Have the Plots Been Exhausted?" Editorial Comment. *Current Literature.* June, '96.

[14] "Rudimentary Suggestions for Beginners in Story Writing," by E. F. Andrews. *Cosmopolitan.* Feb., '97.

[15] For a complete discussion of the proper use of facts in fiction see Chapter V.—THE AUTHOR.

[16] "Rudimentary Suggestions for Beginners in Story Writing," by E. F. Andrews. *Cosmopolitan.* Feb., '97.

[17] "Magazine Fiction and How Not to Write It," by Frederick M. Bird. *Lippincott's.* Nov., '94.

IV

TITLES GOOD AND BAD

Too often the novice considers the title of his story a matter of no import. He looks upon it as a mere handle, the result of some happy afterthought, affixed to the completed story for convenience or reference, just as numbers are placed on the books in a library. The title is really a fair test of what it introduces, and many a MS. has been justly condemned by its title alone; for the editor knows that a poor title usually means a poor story. Think, too, how often you yourself pass a story by with but a casual glance, because its title does not interest you: experience has shown you that you seldom enjoy reading a story which bears an unattractive title.

"A book's name often has an astonishing influence on its first sale. A title that piques curiosity or suggests excitement or emotion will draw a crowd of readers the moment it appears, while a book soberly named must force its merits on the public. The former has all the advantage of a pretty girl over a plain one; it is given an instantaneous chance to prove itself worth while. A middle aged, unalluring title ('In Search of Quiet,' for instance) may frighten people away from what proves to be a mine of wit and human interest. A book headed by a man's name unmodified and uncommented upon—such as 'Horace Chase'—is apt to have a dreary, unprepossessing air, unless the name is an incisive one that suggests an interesting personality. Fragments of proverbs and poems are always attractive, as well as Biblical phrases and colloquial expressions, but the magic title is the one that excites and baffles curiosity. The publishers of a recent 'Primer of Evolution' received a sudden flood of orders for the book simply on account of a review which had spoken of it under the sobriquet, 'From Gas to Genius.' Many copies were indignantly returned when the true title was revealed."[18] "In 1850 Dr. O. M. Mitchell, Director of the Astronomical Observatory in Cincinnati, gave to the press a volume entitled 'The Planetary and Stellar Worlds.' The book fell dead from the press. The publisher complained bitterly of this to a friend, saying, 'I have not sold a single copy.' 'Well,' was the reply, 'you have killed the book by its title. Why not call it "The Orbs of Heaven"?' The hint was accepted and acted upon, and 6,000 copies were sold in a month."[19]

The title might almost be called the "text" of the story; it should be logically deduced from the plot; so a poor title usually indicates a poor plot and a poor story. This name line should grow out of the phase of the plot, rather than the basic theme, else it will be too abstract and general. It is so closely allied to the plot that they should be born synchronously—or if anything the title should precede the plot; for the story is built up around the central thought that the title expresses, much as Poe said he wrote "The Raven" about the word "nevermore." At least, the title should be definitely fixed long before the story is completed, and often before it has taken definite form in the writer's mind. That this is the practice of professional writers may be proved by a glance at the literary column of any periodical, where coming books are announced by title when scarcely a word of them has been written. So if you have difficulty in finding an appropriate title for your story, first examine your plot, and make sure that the cause does not lie there. In case you are unable to decide among a number of possible titles, any one of which might do, you may find that your plot lacks the definiteness of impression required by the short story; but a fertile intellect may suggest a number of good titles, from which your only difficulty is to select the best.

A good story may be given a bad title by its author, and so started toward failure. Novices are peculiarly liable to this fault, usually through allowing themselves to be too easily satisfied. They go to infinite pains to make the story itself fresh and individual, and then cap it with a commonplace phrase that is worse than no title at all. A good title is apt, specific, attractive, new, and short.

A title is apt if it is an outgrowth of the plot—a text, as I have said. It stands definitely for that particular story, and gives a suggestion of what is to come—but only a suggestion, lest it should anticipate the denouement and so satisfy the curiosity of the reader too soon. An apt title excites and piques the curiosity almost as much as does the story itself. Examples: Hawthorne's "The Wedding Knell;" Poe's "'Thou Art the Man!'" Wilkins' "The Revolt of Mother." Each of these titles conveys an idea, though a vague one, of the theme of the story, and so its aptness is apparent; but frequently the relevancy of the title is evident only after the story has been read, as in the case of James' "The Real Thing" and "The Lesson of the Master." Such a title is almost ideal. This suspension of aptness, carried to the extreme, produces such vague and weak titles as:

"Happiness Won."
"Almost Too Late."
"After All."
"Reorganized."

The title must be specific or it is seldom apt. It is in this particular that the novice generally fails. He deduces his title rather from the original plot, or even from the theme, than from the particular phase which he presents; but its title should distinguish his story from the host of tales builded upon the same basic plot, just as the Christian name of a Smith distinguishes him from the rest of the great family of which he is a member. Thus we have such titles as the following, which are more appropriate for essays in psychology, moral philosophy, or some kindred subject, than for fiction:

"How Dreams Come True."
"Moral Vision."

"Sorrow and Joy."
"The Straight Path."

More often the unspecific title is simply a vague reference to the general style of the story:

"A Wedding in a Texas Jail."
"A Frightful Night Ride."
"A Unique Rescue."
"A Lynching Incident."
"Nature's Freaks."
"A Valuable Discovery."
"The Widow."
"A Valued Relic."
"A Strange Case."
"The Old Clock."
"The Office Boy."

None of these titles represents any definite idea, and in nearly every case it served to introduce a story which was equally vague, ordinary, and uninteresting. Several of them, too—notably the first four—were not stories at all, but were simply bits of description by narrative, as their titles would suggest.

In general a phrase, otherwise indefinite, becomes specific when united with the name of a character, as in Hawthorne's "Howe's Masquerade" and "Lady Eleanor's Mantle;" but such titles are usually ordinary and unattractive. Some words frequently found in these compound titles are so vague in meaning or so worn from use that their total avoidance is the only safe course. Such are "Christmas," "Adventure," "Romance," "Story," "Vision," and "Dream." A "Dream" or a "Vision" is usually the relation of some commonplace incident with absurd adornments; and an "Adventure" is more often a piece of description than of narration. I know that these words may be found in combination in many happy titles, but it is best that the novice let them severely alone. That such titles are really a serious impediment to the success of their stories is shown by the action of the Chicago *Record*. For some years it was the custom of the *Record* to offer substantial cash prizes for the best Christmas stories written by school children; and prominent among the rules governing the competition was the announcement that stories bearing such titles as "Johnnie's Christmas," "Nellie's Christmas," "Mary's Christmas," would not even be read. The following titles show how fond is the novice of these objectionable words in their baldest combinations:

"Sarah's Christmas Present."
"Adventures with a Bear."
"Nettie's Romance."
"Lee's Romance."
"A Woman's Love Story."
"The Captain's Story."
"A True Story."
"The Story of a Vision."
"The Dream at Sea."
"Viola's Dream."
"Mabel's Dream."
"Eleanor's Dream."

The title should be attractive because it will be the test of the story, and it must be sufficiently interesting to arouse at a glance the curiosity of the reader, and induce in him a desire to peruse the narrative that it offers. Commonplaceness is the chief cause of the unattractive title, and that fault is usually traceable to the plot itself. It may, however, be due to a conventional expression of the dominant idea of the story, as in the list just given; and also in the following:

"How Amy Won the Prize."
"Fred Norton, the Artist."

Or it may be unattractive through comprising only the name of the chief character:

"Lucy Bonneville."
"Lester Rice."

The use of a name for a title is a matter which it is difficult to settle. If the story is dominated by one character, and particularly if it is a genuine *Character Study*, the writer naturally feels that he cannot do better than to name it after the character it depicts; and he has good authority for so doing in the example of Poe

("Berenice," "Elenora," "Morella"), Hawthorne ("Sylph Etherege," "Ethan Brand," "Wakefield"), Irving ("Wolfert Webber," "Rip Van Winkle"), James ("Sir Dominic Ferrand," "Nona Vincent," "Greville Fane"), Stevenson ("Olalla," "Thrawn Janet," "Markheim"), Wilkins ("Louisa"), Davis ("Gallegher," "Cinderella"), Kipling ("Lispeth," "Namgay Doola"), etc., etc. A good rule to observe would be this: If the name of the chief personage gives a hint of character, or if it is sufficiently unusual to attract attention, it may be used as a title; but in general it will be stronger if used in combination.

In the endeavor to make his title distinctive and attractive the novice is liable to fall into the error of making it cheap and sensational. A title which offends against good taste must not be used, no matter how desirable it may appear in the matter of attractiveness. The newspaper caption writer who headed an account of a hanging "Jerked to Jesus!" attained the acme of attractiveness, but he also committed an unpardonable sin against good taste. The short story writer seldom descends to such depths of sensationalism: his chief offense consists in the use of double titles, connected by the word "or." Often either title alone would be passable, if not really good; but their united form must be placed in the category of bad titles. Such titles are rated as bad chiefly through the effects of association. It used to be common for a story to bear a double title; but to-day the custom has been relegated to the cheap, sensational tale of the "penny dreadful" order, and the conjunctive title is a recognized mark of "yellow" literature. This fault in a title can usually be corrected by the use of either of the titles alone, as may be seen from a study of the following:

(1) "The Story of Dora; or, Innocence Triumphant."

(2) "Jessie Redmond; or, The Spider and the Fly."

(3) "Outwitted; or, The Holdup of No. 4."

(4) "The Battle of the Black Cats; or, A Tragedy Played with Twenty Thousand Actors and Only One Spectator."

(5) "Fate; or, Legend of 'Say Au Revoir, but not Goodbye.'"

(6) "The Romance of a Lost Mine; or, The Curse of the Navajos."

(7) "A Little Bunch of Rosebuds; or, Two Normal Graduates."

(8) "Her Silk Quilt; or, On the Crest of the Wave."

(1) Neither part is particularly happy. "The Story of Dora" is too general, and conveys an idea of largeness and time that is better suited to the novel than to the short story; "Innocence Triumphant" is cheap, sensational and trite. (2) "Jessie Redmond" is too commonplace a name to be a good head line; "The Spider and the Fly" was worn out years ago. (3) Either title alone is good; "The Holdup of No. 4" is preferable because of its definiteness. (4) "The Battle of the Black Cats" alone would pass, in spite of its hint of sensationalism; but the second part is of course ludicrously impossible. (5) "Fate" is too indefinite; the second title is cheap and old. (6) Either would do, though the first is somewhat vague, and "Curse" savors of sensationalism. (7) Either would do, though the first sounds rather silly. (8) The first is good; the second is vague and rather old.

That a title should be new is so obvious that offenses against this rule are usually unconscious; yet in some cases stories have been capped with stolen headings, where the theft was so apparently intentional that it seemed as if the writer wished to fail. Lapses in this regard are usually due to the writer's ignorance of the value of a title; or to the too ready use of the abstract theme, as mentioned before. Of such titles are "All's Well that Ends Well," "Love's Labor Lost," and "The Irony of Fate," all of which are great favorites with the beginner. Like charity, they will cover a multitude of sins, but they constitute so great a literary sin in themselves that they should be rigorously eschewed. To this class belongs also such a title as "Cuba Libre!" which is so very old, and which during the last few years has been so twisted and mishandled in every conceivable way that its mere use is an irritation. Such a title will frequently be apt, specific, attractive, and, in application, new; but it will so exasperate the reader that its use will be perilous.

For self-evident reasons the title should be short. Aptness and specificness do not require an epitome of the story; and a title like "Why Tom Changed His Opinion of Me," or "What the Rabbit Drive Did for Me" is prosy as well as long. It used to be the custom to make the title of a writing a regular synopsis of the matter contained therein; but modern readers object to being told in advance exactly what is to happen. No ruling concerning the proper length of a short story title is possible; but generally speaking, the shorter the title the better it is. Compound titles connected by "or," like those previously mentioned, are as offensive in their length as in their sensationalism.

To illustrate further these several points I introduce here a few good titles used by successful short story writers. They are roughly divided into three classes according to their derivation. The title may be the text of the story:

Edgeworth: "Murad the Unlucky."

Hawthorne: "The Wedding Knell;" "The Prophetic Pictures."

James: "The Real Thing;" "The Lesson of the Master."

Poe: "The Masque of the Red Death;" "'Thou Art the Man!'"

Stockton: "The Transferred Ghost."

Wilkins: "The Revolt of Mother;" "Two Old Lovers."

The title may represent the principal character by name or by some apt appellation:

Davis: "Gallegher."

Hawthorne: "The Ambitious Guest;" "Feathertop."

Irving: "The Spectre Bridegroom;" "Rip Van Winkle."

Poe: "Morella;" "Ligeia."

Stevenson: "Markheim."

Wilkins: "A Modern Dragon;" "A Kitchen Colonel."

The title may mention the principal object:

Adee: "The Life Magnet."

Burnett: "The Spider's Eye."

Hawthorne: "The Great Stone Face;" "The Great Carbuncle."

James: "The Aspern Papers."

Kipling: "The Phantom 'Rickshaw."

Poe: "The Black Cat;" "The Gold Bug."

Stevenson: "The Bottle Imp."

THE USE OF FACTS

ALL fiction is founded upon fact, for the boldest imagination must have some definite point from which to take its flight; but the ungarnished truth is seldom literature in itself, though it may offer excellent material for literary embellishment. The amateur, content with knowing that he is recounting what did actually happen, falls into the most inartistic ways, because he does not understand that facts are properly only crude material for the fictionist.

The one place where the average short story writer should *not* seek his material is the world of literature. Almost from the time when men first began to dabble in letters they have drawn on their predecessors for their subject matter; but this practice has produced a deal of unconscious plagiarism, which is responsible for most of the conventional and stereotyped stories with which we are afflicted to-day. Of any one hundred average stories submitted for sale, probably seventy-five are damned by their hopelessly hackneyed conception and treatment; and they suffer because the writer, reading some attractive story built upon a similar plot, has attempted to go and do likewise, and has unconsciously used all the conventional parts while omitting the essential individuality.

It is safe for the novice to go only to the world for literary material. The matter so obtained will be intrinsically the same as that gained from the writings of others, but the fact that you get your information through your own senses will considerably obviate the danger of adopting the conventional view in the matter. I do not mean to say that you should deliberately set out to search for new types and incidents as Dickens did, though I would certainly commend such a course; I mean rather that you should be content to write of what you personally and intimately know, and not attempt to treat of matters of which you have only a vague superficial knowledge, or of which you are totally ignorant. Excellent stories have been written by men who were personally unacquainted with the matters with which they dealt, but they were in every case masters of their art, who knew how to gain and use second-hand information and how to supplement insufficient data with literary skill.

Too many novices have the mistaken idea that only those things which are dim and distant are fit for artistic treatment. They have not cultivated their powers of perception, and have failed to grasp the truth that human nature is in most respects the same the world over, and that persons and places, apparently the most ordinary, have stories to tell. Before Mary E. Wilkins began to write her New England tales few thought to look to those bleak hills and commonplace people for literary material; and doubtless many New Englanders, feeling the impulse to write, viewed with scorn their unpoetic surroundings and longed for the glamour of some half-guessed clime; Miss Wilkins, appreciating her environment, won fame and fortune through her truthful depictions of those things which others, equally able to write but less able to see, had despised.

It is a common trick of aspiring writers to locate their stories in England, to speak proudly but uncertainly of grand estates, noble castles, and haughty lords and ladies, and to make mistakes which would be ridiculous were they not so inexcusable. There is a certain half-feudal glamour about England yet which appeals strongly to the callow author: it lends that rosy haze of romance and unreality which is popularly associated with fiction; but it was long ago done to death by mediocre writers and laughed out of good literary society, and to-day America will not suffer any such hackneyed fol-de-rol.

Similarly the amateur will locate his story in the "best" society of some American metropolis, when he has never been out of his native village, and knows nothing of the class with which he deals except through the society column of his newspaper. Therefore he will of course "fall flat when he attempts to delineate manners. It is too evident that he has not had the *entree* to the circle he would describe: his gentlemen commit too many blunders, his ladies are from the wrong side of the town, the love-passages are silly and vulgar, the whole result is stupid and offensive—to those who know. The thing hopelessly lacks tone; it might pass below stairs, but not in the drawing-room."[20] It is not only those of wealth and leisure who are eligible for literary purposes; indeed, their lives, apparently so gay and exciting, are often a dull and regular series of attempts to kill the dawdling time. If the young writer would look into the lives of his own simple neighbors he would find much better matter for his intended stories.

Again, the novice, in his search for something different, will place his tale in the dim and distant past, when all men were brave and all women lovely; and in so doing will expose himself to ridicule and contempt for his evident ignorance of the matters of which he pretends to treat. It is very probable that any age seems dull and commonplace to those who live in it, for "familiarity breeds contempt" for almost anything; but though we of to-day have no valiant knights, armed cap-a-pie, riding forth to the jousts to do battle for their ladies fair, we have men just as brave and deeds fully as valorous and far more sensible; and the world is, and always will be, full of noble and romantic and marvelous things.

If, however, you feel that you must write of times and scenes and peoples which are either past or foreign, it is your first duty to inform yourself to the best of your ability concerning them. I do not believe that any writer can successfully locate his story in a foreign country unless he has personal knowledge of the scenes and persons that he describes, or unless he is thoroughly versed in the language and literature of the country—and in the latter case he would probably be too pedantic to write readable stories. At first thought it does not seem so difficult to handle English subjects, for there we have the advantage of a common language and, to a considerable extent, of common racial traits; but even that common language, as spoken on the other side of the Atlantic, has an every-day vocabulary differing from ours, and the English government and social system present difficulties almost insurmountable to one who cannot study them face to face. In dealing with themes of the past there is more opportunity. There we are all on the common ground of an absolute dependence on such books as may preserve for us pictures of those times, and complete information—complete, at least, in the sense that no one knows more—can be had at the price of a certain number of hours of painstaking study. If, then, you desire to write of the days that are gone, see to it that you first thoroughly acquaint yourself with the history of those times. There are few towns too small to possess a library, and few libraries too small to contain such historical books as you may need.

In these days when all things come to Mohamet, the writer may gain a valuable though impersonal insight into the world at large through the medium of the public press. The newspapers of to-day are full of incipient plots, needing only the skillful pen to make them literature. Reporters go everywhere and see everything, and they place the result of their multifarious labors in your hands every morning. They recount actual happenings accurately enough for literary purposes, they strain for the unusual side of things, and their purpose is too different from yours to make you liable to the charge of plagiarism if you rework their material. The receptive perusal of any newspaper ought to furnish the reader with a fresh stock of literary material. Such matter is particularly valuable to the short story writer because of the present and ever increasing demand for stories of the day, plots, characters, situations, and local color for which may be culled from any newspaper.

But short story writing is an art, and all facts may not be capable of literary treatment. "Even actual occurrences may be improper subjects for fiction. Nature can take liberties with facts that art dare not—a truth that has passed into a proverb.... Art may fill us with anger, fear, terror, awe, but the moment it condescends to excite disgust, it passes out of the realm of art." [21] "There seems no reason why the artist should not choose any subject, if the production itself contributes to the satisfaction of the world, making a picture of life, or of a phase of life, in compliance with the demands of art, beauty, and truth. Taste is the arbiter of the subject, for taste is always moral, always on the side of the angels. There are certain things which are only subjects for technical reform, for the sanitary inspector, and for the physician—not for the novelist."[22] "The carnage of a battle-field, the wrecked café or theatre after dynamite has done its work, had best be handled sparingly.... A good many things that happen on this planet are not good subjects for art: the pathetic (within limits) is always in order, but not the shocking. Moral are worse than physical horrors."[23] "Even genius may waste itself on an unmanageable theme; it cannot make the cleaning of fish interesting, nor the slums of New York or Paris attractive."[24]

It is rare indeed that a fact can be used without embellishment. Mere facts are frequently most unliterary, though they may be susceptible of a high literary polish. The sub-title "A True Story," which young writers think so valuable a part of the tale, is too often the trademark of an unreadable mess of conventional people, ordinary incidents and commonplace conversation. We find few genuinely true stories, and when we do find them we seldom care to read them through. I have read many stories which I knew to be literally true, because they contained so much of the hackneyed and the irrelevant. Life itself is a very conventional affair; it abounds with dull events and stupid people; and for that reason alone fiction would demand something out of the common. Commonplace persons and commonplace things do appear in literature, but they must have something more than their commonplaceness to recommend them.

"The novice in story telling ... has heard that truth is stranger than fiction, and supposes that the more truth he can get into his tale the stronger and more effective it will be.... Truth, *i. e.*, reality, is very seldom strange; it is usually tame and flat and commonplace; and when it is strange it is apt to be grotesque and repulsive. Most of the experiences of daily life afford material only for a chronicle of dulness; and most of the 'strange' or unusual happenings had better be left to the newspaper and the records of the police courts. This statement may be strengthened. Does not the able reporter select and decorate his facts, suppressing some, emphasizing others, arranging his 'story' with reference to picturesqueness and effect?

"In other words, verisimilitude, not verity, is wanted in fiction. The observer notes his facts, and then the artist seizes on the ideas behind them, the types they represent, the spiritual substances they embody. The result, when all goes well, is as lifelike as life itself, though it is not a copy of anything (in detail) that really lives.... The budding writer of fictitious tales must be familiar with facts, at least in his own range: he must know life and nature, or his work is naught. But when he has this knowledge, he must put the facts in the background of his mind.... Real incidents, dragged against their will into an (alleged) imaginary narrative, are apt by no means to improve it, but to sound as 'flat and untunable' as our own praises from our own mouths."[25]

"There must be no misconception about great fiction being a transcript of life. Mere transcription is not the work of an artist, else we should have no need of painters, for photographers would do; no poems, for academical essays would do; no great works of fiction, for we have our usual sources of information—if information is all we want—the Divorce Court, the Police Court, the Stock Exchange, the Young Ladies' Seminary, the

Marriage Register, and the House of Parliament—those happy hunting-grounds of sensation-mongers and purveyors of melodrama. All these things certainly contain the facts of life which one must know for the constructive work of the imagination, for they are the rough material, the background of knowledge from which the illusion of real life must proceed. But they are not life, though they are the transcription of life. The human significance of facts is all that concerns one. The inwardness of facts makes fiction; the history of life, its emotions, its passions, its sins, reflections, values. These you cannot photograph nor transcribe. Selection and rejection are two profound essentials of every art, even of the art of fiction, though it be so jauntily practised by the amateur."[26]

And even if the facts which you purpose to use are of undoubted value for artistic treatment, there may be other reasons which make their use questionable. In the first place, people do not really prefer truth to fiction. They require plausibility, but they are all too familiar with life themselves, and in the idle hours in which they turn to fiction they desire to be lifted out of reality into the higher realm of fancy. Nor will they, even in the form of fiction, tolerate what seems like too gross an invasion of the privacy of the home, or the sanctity of the soul of a man. They must always feel vaguely that the suffering characters are really only puppets created for their amusement, or their pity for the characters will develop into anger and disgust for the author.

In using facts, then, the first thing to learn is what to suppress and what to elaborate, and that involves that most necessary possession of the story teller, a sense of proportion. Because a conversation about the weather occupies two dull people for ten minutes is no reason that it should receive an equal number of pages; and because an important event is almost instantaneous is no excuse for passing it with a single line. Again, the fact that you are relating what actually occurred does not relieve you of the necessity of making it plausible. Painters acknowledge that there are color combinations in nature which they dare not reproduce, lest they be dubbed unnatural; and similarly things exist which the writer may present only after he has most carefully prepared the way for their credence. The truth is that we have declared that even nature shall conform to certain conventions, and we reject as impossible any deviations from our preconceived ideas.

The facts upon which Hawthorne built "The Ambitious Guest" are these:—The White Hills of which he speaks (¶ 1) are the famous White Mountains of New Hampshire; the Notch (¶ 1) is the real name of a real mountain pass, which is just as he describes it; the Flume (¶ 22) is a waterfall not far from the Notch; the valley of the Saco (¶ 1) is really where he places it. The references to Portland (¶ 3), Bartlett (¶ 5), Burlington (¶ 7), Bethlehem and Littleton (¶ 18) are all references to real places in the vicinity. At the point where Hawthorne locates his story there actually was a mountain tavern called the Willey House, and a modern inn stands on the spot to-day. Concerning the catastrophe which he describes I found the following account:

"Some time in June—before the great 'slide' in August, 1826—there came a great storm, and the old veteran, Abel Crawford, coming down the Notch, noticed the trees slipping down, standing upright, and, as he was passing Mr. Willey's he called and informed him of the wonderful fact. Immediately, in a less exposed place, Mr. Willey prepared a shelter to which to flee in case of immediate danger; and in the night of August 28th, that year, he was, with his family, awakened by the thundering crash of the coming avalanche. Attempting to escape, that family, nine in number, rushed from the house and were overtaken and buried alive under a vast pile of rocks, earth, trees and water. By a remarkable circumstance the house remained uninjured, as the slide divided about four rods back of the house (against a high flat rock), and came down on either side with overwhelming power."[27]

The book goes on to state further that the family consisted of the father and mother, five children—the eldest a girl of thirteen—and two hired men. The bodies of the parents, the oldest and youngest children, and the two hired men were found.

It is probable that Hawthorne derived his information from the newspapers, though he may have heard the story by word of mouth, for there is little doubt that he actually visited the spot where the catastrophe occurred. But the bald facts of the case, however gained, are essentially as we have them here, and that is sufficient for our purpose.

In writing his story Hawthorne took several liberties with the facts. He made no change in the location because even he could not improve upon the scene for such a story. He changed the month from August to September (¶ 1) to make plausible, perhaps, the rain necessary for such a slide, and to make seasonable the bitter wind which he introduces. He omitted all names to add to the air of unsolved mystery that haunts the story. He introduced the guest (¶ 4) and the grandmother (¶ 1), increased the age of the daughter (¶ 1), retained the parents and younger children (¶ 1) and omitted the hired men to suit the requirements of his story. He omitted the warning but retained the establishment of a place of refuge (¶ 9) to heighten the climax. He used the flight from the house (¶ 42) because it just suited his purpose. He retained the strange preservation of the house (¶ 42) to increase the air of mystery, and to intensify the tragedy by making it appear in a manner unnecessary. He suppressed the finding of any of the bodies (¶ 42) to aid the plausibility of his narrative, and to increase the pathos of the guest's death.

Compare carefully the account given by Spaulding and the story of Hawthorne, for you have here an excellent illustration of the difference between the commonplace recital of facts and their transformation into a work of art. Spaulding's relation is a true story, but Hawthorne's is literature.

FOOTNOTES:

[20] "Bad Story-Telling," by Frederick M. Bird. *Lippincott's*. Oct., '97.

[21] "Rudimentary Suggestions for Beginners in Story Writing," by E. F. Andrews. *Cosmopolitan*. Feb., '97.

[22] "The Art of Fiction." A lecture by Gilbert Parker. *The Critic*. Dec., '98.

[23] "Magazine Fiction and How Not to Write It," by Frederick M. Bird. *Lippincott's*. Nov., '94.

[24] "Bad Story-Telling," by Frederick M. Bird. *Lippincott's*, Oct., '97.

[25] "Fact in Fiction," by Frederick M. Bird. *Lippincott's*, July, '95.

[26] "The Art of Fiction." A lecture by Gilbert Parker. *The Critic*. Dec., '98.

[27] "Historical Relics of the White Mountains," by John H. Spaulding. (Boston, 1855.) "Destruction of the Willey Family," page 58.

VI

THE CHARACTERS

It is the tritest sort of a truism to say that the characters in a story are important, for stories are stories only in so far as they reflect life, and life is impossible without human actors. It is the hopes and fears, the joys and sorrows, the sins and moral victories of men that interest us. We men are a conceited lot, and find nothing of interest except as it relates to us. Thus in the most ingenious stories, where some marvelous invention or discovery is introduced, the interest centers, not in the wondrous things themselves, but in their influence on the people of the story; and in the few stories where a beast or a thing plays the hero, it is always given human attributes.

Fictitious characters, like the plots that they develop, are based primarily on fact, and they further resemble the plots in being different phases of a primal idea, rather than intrinsically diverse. We find many characters in fiction—Miss Wilkins' stories are full of them—which are evidently meant to be realistic, and which impress us as word photographs of existing persons; yet it is improbable that they are exact reproductions. A real person ordinarily has too much of the commonplace and conventional about him to serve in fiction, where—despite the apparent paradox—a character must be exaggerated to appear natural. A person in fiction is at the best but a blur of hieroglyphics on a sheet of paper, and can be comprehended only through the mentality of the author; therefore his description, his actions, his words, his very thoughts must be made so unnaturally striking that through the sense of sight alone they will stimulate the imagination and produce the effect which actual contact with the real person would induce. The character which seems most real is usually a composite of the most striking characteristics of several real persons. To this source of fictitious characters is due the fact that a literary puppet is often thought to be the reproduction of several very different real persons; for the reader, recognizing a particular trait which is characteristic of some one of his acquaintance, thinks that he recognizes the character.

"While the popular idea that every creature of the novelist's imagination has a definite original somewhere among his acquaintances is, of course, egregiously false, it has yet this much of truth, that they are, to a large extent, suggestions from life. Not one person, but half a dozen, often sit as models for the same picture, while the details are filled out by the writer's imagination. There are few people in real life sufficiently interesting or uncommonplace to suit the novelist's purpose, but he must idealize or intensify them before they are fit subjects for art. Dickens intensified to the verge of the impossible, yet we never feel that Dick Swiveller and Sam Weller and Mr. Micawber, and the rest of them, are unnatural; they are only, if I may coin the word, 'hypernatural.' It is the business of art to idealize. Even at its best art is so inferior to nature, that in order to produce the same impression it has to intensify its effects; to deepen the colors, heighten the contrasts, omit an object here, exaggerate an outline there, and so on, until it has produced the proper picturesque effect."[28]

A careful description of the appearance of the characters may be necessary to the understanding of the story, as in Irving's perfect picture of Ichabod Crane in "The Legend of Sleepy Hollow"; but in our model the people are rather typical than individual, and Hawthorne devotes but little space to their external characteristics. A word or a phrase suffices to tell us all that is necessary to enable our minds to body them forth. Even the hero is outwardly distinguished only by a melancholy expression—a slight of which no school-girl "authoress" would have been guilty. It is more often necessary to give the mental characteristics of the puppets, and in "The Ambitious Guest" we have a deal of such detail concerning the young stranger; but here, too, you must exercise forbearance, as Hawthorne did in his partial analysis of the other characters.

It is by no means essential that the personages of a short story be attractive in person or in character. The taste of readers used to be so artificial that no romancer would have dared to present a heroine who was not perfect in face and figure, or a hero who was not an Apollo for manly beauty; but in these more practical days we have substituted good deeds for good looks and have made our characters more human—our men more manly and our women more womanly; and we exalt them now for heroic acts, rather than heroic mould.

A mistake which it seems hard for the novice to avoid is that of telling everything possible about a character and leaving nothing to the imagination of the reader. This exhaustive method leads to a multiplicity of detail which verges on baldness, and which is very apt to contain considerable irrelevant matter; the details are usually arranged with little regard for their true value; and the intended description becomes a mere catalogue of personal charms. For example, in these three descriptions, detailed though they are, there is nothing to distinguish the particular person described from the scores of other people possessing the same general traits:

> He was a tall, deep-chested, broad-shouldered man, having a light complexion, dark moustache, hair and eyes.

> We will take a look at our heroine, as she sits lazily rocking, the sunshine touching her hair. She is of medium height, with black hair and eyes and a winning smile that makes friends for her everywhere.

> Lura was yet but a slight school girl; she was now fifteen and equally as large as Grace. She looked very beautiful as she came out to meet Grace and Mrs. Morton, on their return from the village. Her dark brown hair had been carefully combed back, but the short locks had fallen and formed in ringlets about the snowy neck and face. Her large gray eyes were bright. Her full curved lips were red, and in laughing and talking revealed two rows of small, even, pearly white teeth. Her cheeks were round and well formed; although at the present time they bore no marks of roses, they were generally

rosy. The gray eyes, by the changing of the expression, often became almost black and greatly completed her beauty.

Clever character depiction consists in selecting and presenting only those salient details which will serve to body forth rather a vague image, which shall yet possess a definite personality, to which the reader may give such distinctness as his imagination may impart to the hints offered. It is in a manner building a complete character upon a single characteristic, after the familiar method of Dickens. It is this impressionistic method which is most used by masters to picture those characters which seem to us real persons.

In "The Legend of Sleepy Hollow," Irving thus describes the hero (?), Ichabod Crane, and the heroine, Katrina Van Tassel:

> The cognomen of Crane was not inapplicable to his person. He was tall, but exceedingly lank, with narrow shoulders, long arms and legs, hands that dangled a mile out of his sleeves, feet that might have served for shovels, and his whole frame most loosely hung together. His head was small, and flat at the top, with huge ears, large green glassy eyes, and a long snipe nose, so that it looked like a weather-cock, perched upon his spindle neck, to tell which way the wind blew. To see him striding along the profile of a hill on a windy day, with his clothes bagging and fluttering about him, one might have mistaken him for the genius of famine descending upon the earth, or some scarecrow eloped from a cornfield.

> She was a blooming lass of fresh eighteen, plump as a partridge, ripe and melting and rosy-cheeked as one of her father's peaches, and universally famed, not merely for her beauty, but her vast expectations. She was withal a little of a coquette, as might be perceived even in her dress, which was a mixture of ancient and foreign fashions, as most suited to set off her charms. She wore the ornaments of pure yellow gold which her great-great-grandmother had brought over from Saardam, the tempting stomacher of the olden time, and withal a provokingly short petticoat to display the prettiest foot and ankle in the country round.

Here are Hawthorne's pictures of Beatrice and her father in "Rappaccini's Daughter":

> On again beholding Beatrice the young man was even startled to perceive how much her beauty exceeded his recollection of it—so brilliant, so vivid in its character, that she glowed amid the sunlight, and, as Giovanni whispered to himself, positively illuminated the more shadowy intervals of the garden path. Her face being now more revealed than on the former occasion, he was struck by its expression of simplicity and sweetness—qualities that had not entered into his idea of her character, and which made him ask anew what manner of mortal she might be. Nor did he fail again to

observe or imagine an analogy between the beautiful girl and the gorgeous shrub that hung its gem-like flowers over the fountain—a resemblance which Beatrice seemed to have indulged a fantastic humor in heightening both by the arrangement of her dress and the selection of its hues.

His figure soon emerged into view, and showed itself to be that of no common laborer, but a tall, emaciated, sallow and sickly-looking man dressed in a scholar's garb of black. He was beyond the middle term of life, with gray hair, and a thin gray beard and a face singularly marked with intellect and cultivation, but which could never, even in his more youthful days, have expressed much warmth of heart.

And this is the way Dickens sets forth Scrooge, the old miser, in "A Christmas Carol":

Oh! But he was a tight-fisted hand at the grindstone, Scrooge! a squeezing, wrenching, grasping, scraping, clutching, covetous, old sinner! Hard and sharp as flint, from which no steel had ever struck out generous fire; secret, and self-contained, and solitary as an oyster. The cold within him froze his old features, nipped his pointed nose, shrivelled his cheek, stiffened his gait, made his eyes red, his thin lips blue; and spoke out shrewdly in his grating voice. A frosty rime was on his head, and on his eyebrows, and his wiry chin. He carried his own low temperature always about with him; he iced his office in the dog-days; and didn't thaw it one degree at Christmas.

There is very little of the catalogue style of description here; indeed, the characters can hardly be said to be described: the author gives rather the sensations which they produced on observers and so excites similar sensations in the mind of the reader.

When once introduced the characters should be allowed to work out their identities with the least possible interference from the author. Their characteristics must not be listed like invoices of goods: they must themselves display the psychological powers with which they were endowed by their creator. Their speeches and actions must seem the results of mental processes, and must appear natural, if not logical; indeed, it is an open question if they can be both at once, for there are few people who are always logical. One good method of presenting the characteristics of a fictitious personage is to indulge in a bit of mind reading, and give his thoughts as he thinks them; another and better way is to show the man actuated by his dominant mental qualities. In "The Cask of Amontillado" Poe builds a whole story on an elaboration of the latter method, and presents the picture of a man temporarily mastered by the spirit of revenge. It is only by thus allowing the characters to work out their own destinies that you can make them real; otherwise they will appear as mere painted puppets, without life or volition.

On account of the technical limitations of the short story the number of characters which may have principal or "speaking" parts is very small—in general only two, and frequently but one. There are usually other characters present to help out the action, but they are merely supernumeraries, without form, life or influence. There are many violations of this rule, I admit, among them such stories as Hawthorne's "The Great Stone Face," "The Seven Vagabonds," and "The Great Carbuncle;" but analysis shows them to be panoramic or episodic in effect, and really violating the unity of action which the short story demands. For similar reasons the characters presented must be unnaturally isolated, with little past and less future, and most strangely lacking in relatives; for the few thousand words of the short story permit but a cursory treatment of the ancestry, birth, breeding and family of the one or two important characters. If by any trick they can be made the last of a long line, and be snatched from obscurity into the momentary glare of the lime light, so much the better for author, reader and character; but if some portion of their history bears upon the story, let it be presented by subtle touches, preferably by references in the dialogue, so that the reader obtains the necessary knowledge without being conscious of the means.

The few real characters in the story must be made unusually interesting on account of their loneliness. They compose the story, they represent the human race, and if they fail us we are in sad straits. They must be individual; they must stand out sharply from the page, clear and attractive, and leave no doubt of their personalities. More than any other form of fiction, the short story depends upon its hero and heroine, who have "star parts" and monopolize the stage of action. We must see them so vividly that when they speak and act we shall perceive them as actual personages. It is such accuracy of depiction that makes Rip Van Winkle, Sherlock Holmes, Van Bibber, and a host of others enter into our thoughts and speech as if they had really lived.

The names with which we label these dolls may be of importance. In these days names have little significance, yet we still feel that a name from its very sound may be appropriate or otherwise, and no careful writer would give to his characters appellations selected at random. Names are frequently used to good advantage as aids to character depiction or to enhance humorous effects, as in the case of Hawthorne's Feathertop and Monsieur du Miroir, and Irving's Ichabod Crane, and in many other instances familiar to readers of Dickens.

"Dickens's names are marvelously apt, as we see from the passing into common phrase of so many of them. Not a few have become synonyms for the kind of character to which they were attached.... If a name is to hint at character it should do so in the subtlest manner possible—in a manner so subtle as to escape all but the quickwitted, who will forgive the inartistic method in their pride at being so clever as to detect the writer's intention.... In these days, when craftsmanship is cared for and looked for more than ever, ... novelists must sacrifice nothing that will lend a trick of reality to their imaginings. If they take any pains to select names for their characters they should hit upon such as will be seen to suit them when their books have been read (like Sir Willoughby Patterne or Gabriel Oak); names that attempt with clumsy impertinence to give a clew to character at the outset are best left to the inept amateur of letters who has not wit enough to dispense with such aid.

"To be avoided, also, are out-of-the-way names that may have living owners in the real world. No John Smith or Tom Jones can complain if writers christen their characters after them; but if a man owns a peculiar name he dislikes having it borrowed and attached to some figure in fiction whose proceedings very likely do it little credit.... Every writer must know the satisfaction that comes when an 'exquisitely right' name is hit upon. But it is just as well to take reasonable precautions to avoid indignant protests such as that which Hawthorne drew upon himself"[29] for his use of the name Judge Pyncheon in "The House of the Seven Gables."

The dramatic trend of the short story is responsible for its tendency to advance action by speech. Good short stories have been written and will be written which contain little or no dialogue; they succeed through vividness of plot, skill in character depiction, ingenuity of construction, or some such quality; but they would be more interesting and more natural if they held more conversation. A short story should be full of talk of the proper kind; there are few people who preserve silence at all times, and in the exciting moments which a short story usually presents, most persons would find tongue to voice their teeming thoughts. Speech adds naturalness and vividness to the actors, it lends them a personal interest, it gives insight into character, and it aids the development of the plot.

This is a modern tendency, for the stories of Kipling, Stevenson, Wilkins, Davis and Doyle contain much more of the conversational element than those of Poe, Hawthorne or Irving. Where the latter would present a mental struggle or a crisis by some paragraphs of description, the former express it in the short exciting words of the actors themselves; even soliloquies and asides and other of the most mechanical devices of the drama are forced into the service of the short story, to replace the long explanatory passages such as were used by Irving. It has been predicted that in the short story of the future the characters will be briefly introduced and then will be allowed to speak for themselves; if this prophecy comes true we shall have stories similar to Hope's "The Dolly Dialogues," or Howells' little dramas, where there is almost no comment by the author. It is more probable, though, that there is something of a "fad" in the present liking for pure dialogue, and that the short story will never attain the absolute purity of the drama.

If these fictitious personages are to talk, however, they must talk naturally and interestingly—and "there's the rub!" As in real life a man often shows himself to be a fool when he begins to talk, so in fiction a character frequently proves to be but a poor puppet of straw when he opens his mouth. The only way to make your characters talk naturally is to imitate the speech of the persons whom they in some degree represent. People in general do not talk by book: they use colloquial language, full of poor grammar, slang, and syncopated words; and their sentences are neither always logical nor complete. In reproducing this, however, you must "edit" it a little, using your own judgment as to which are the characteristic idioms; for the speech of the people in books is admittedly a little better than in real life—except in dialect stories, where it is usually worse; and you must avoid equally the heavy rhetorical style of the extreme romantic school, and the inane commonplaces of the radical realists.

Conversation like the following is commonly termed "bookish"; it is painfully correct and laboriously profound—but it is not natural. If it were meant for a burlesque upon polite and "cultured" society it would be exquisite, but it is the manner in which the writer believes people really talk, though it is easy to guess that he himself is far from such absurd affectations in his familiar speech.

"By way of preliminary, I have to say that my name is Athlee—Felix Athlee, and yours is Miss India Lemare. I've seen you before."

"In the flesh, I hope," she answered.

"Yes, I like you better that way, though you now wear the expression of one older in years and experience. Wherefore, may I ask?"

"Shadows fall on the young as well as the old. One is fortunate, indeed, to keep always in the sunshine."

"And flit like the butterfly, without volition or effort? Human appointments are different. Work is the inevitable, and with the proper tools, it is pleasant enough."

"They must, long ago, have rusted, for the want of use."

"No, we have simply to consider our specialty and we find them ready at hand. Have you done so?"

"I am dazed, and my brain works capriciously."

"Except in the interest of your desires. What are they?"

"Wealth for independence, leisure for indulgence, and fame, the outcome of talent."

His luminous eyes looked out over the water, as he said: "The universal hunt of mankind is for happiness, and he searches for it in as many ways as there are peculiarities of disposition. Does he ever really find it? Many weary hearts are covered with the soft down of wealth. Mischief lurks in indulgence, and fame dazzles but to elude. It is wiser to accept what the gods give, and use the gifts for the betterment of others as well as ourselves."

"Meaningless words, when one is at enmity with the gods for withholding. What fine spun theories we mortals have!"

To the listener every conversation contains a deal of commonplace: it may be that the speakers really have nothing interesting to say, and it may be that their conversation is so personal as to interest themselves only. The reader occupies the position of a listener, and it is the duty of the author to suppress all commonplace dialogue, unless, as sometimes happens, it assists in plot or character development. Conversation like the following is—let us hope—interesting to the parties concerned, but the reader would be delivered from it as from a plague.

"I am so glad to get *one* desire of my heart."

"And that is?" said Al.

"Snow!"

"So glad that is all. I thought you had spied my new tie and was planning some 'crazy design' upon it."

"Oh, let me see! Now, really, that is becoming to your style, but I think it would suit mine better. 'Brown eyes and black hair should never wear blue—that is for grey eyes, the tried and true.' See?"

"Neither the eyes nor the tie," said Al, as he turned his back and looked up at the ceiling.

The real difficulty with this dialogue is that the writer attempted to make his characters "smart" and so permitted them to indulge in repartee; but as they were only commonplace people the privilege was too much for them and they merely twaddled. They did succeed in being humorous, but the humor is unconscious.

Yet unconscious humor is preferable to the forced and desperate attempt at fun-making which we have in this extract:

"I don't believe he is proud," said Joe to Tom, his younger brother. "But you know he has been to the Holy Land and cannot now associate with such wicked sinners as we are. Or else he has turned Jew and thinks we are Samaritans."

"You two are getting no better fast," said the doctor, after a hearty laugh. "Wait until you get sick, I'll give you a pill that will make you repent."

"We are never going to get sick," said Joe, "but expect to live until we are so old that we will dry up and blow away with the wind, or go to heaven in a 'Chariot of Fire.'" Turning to the doctor Joe continued: "You know Will has a girl, and he is awful pious. If one looks off his book in church, even to wink at his best girl, he thinks it an awful sin. And that the guilty one should be dipped in holy water, or do penitence for a week."

It is a common trick for the novice to put into the mouths of his characters just such stale jokes and cheap jests, with the idea that he is doing something extremely funny. He is, but his audience is laughing at him, not at his characters.

But most exasperating of all is the author who, while making his characters suffer the most dreadful afflictions, lets them think and talk only commonplaces still, like the poor sawdust dolls that they are:

"What is the matter with you, Annie?" I said one day, about five months after she had come home....

"You will know some time, Cicely," she answered....

"Why can't you tell me now?" I asked.

"You will know soon enough," she answered. "By the by," she went on, "I am going to Mr. Denham's to-morrow."

"Alone?"

"No, I am going with Cousin Ivan."

"When will you be back?" I asked, for Mr. Denham lived twenty miles away.

"I don't know," she answered sadly.

The next morning I went over to see Annie off. I had been there but a few minutes when her cousin, Ivan Carleon, came. He was about six feet high, with dark, brown eyes, and black hair and moustache. He was a quiet man and I liked him. When they got ready to start, Annie came and kissed me.

"I am ready now, Ivan." And then he helped her into the buggy, and they drove off.

Two days afterwards, as I was sitting under the shade of a tree, where Annie and I had played when we were small, Miss Jones, an old school fellow, came along.

"Have you heard the news?" she asked, before she had got up to me.

"What news?"

"Why, Ivan Carleon has killed Annie."

"Explain yourself, Daisy," I answered anxiously.

"Well," she said, "we ain't sure Ivan killed her; but every one thinks so. You know that big gate, about a mile this side of Mr. Denham's? Well, day before yesterday Ivan came running up to Mr. Denham, and said that Annie had shot herself, down at the big gate. They all went down and found Annie stone dead. A note in her pocket merely stated that she was tired of life. But every one thinks Ivan killed her, and that he wrote the note himself. I hope Ivan didn't do it," she said, as she started off, "for I liked him."

The evening of the third day, as I was sitting under the same tree, I was startled to feel a hand on my shoulder. Looking up, I saw Ivan Carleon standing by my side. I gave a low cry, and shrank from him. He turned pale to his lips.

"Surely you don't think I murdered her?" he said.

"I don't know what to think," I answered, bursting into tears.

"Sit down and tell me all about it," I continued, moving for him on the bench.

He sat down beside me; and laid his head in his hands.

Imagine, if you can, the bearer of terrible news who would unburden herself with as little excitement as Miss Jones exhibits; or a real girl who, on hearing of the tragic death of her bosom friend, would be merely "anxious" and bid her informant "Explain yourself!" The author of this could not have had the slightest conception of the tragedy which he had created, or even his poor lifeless puppets must have been galvanized into some show of real feeling.

It is neither necessary nor desirable that you should report every conversation at length, even though it bear upon the story. Do not reproduce long conversations simply to say something or to air your views on current topics. It is just as much a fault to introduce useless chatter as it is to fill page after page with descriptions of unused places. If the hero and the heroine, by a brief bright conversation, can put the reader in possession of the facts concerning the course of their true love, they should be given free speech; but if they show a tendency to moralize or prose or talk an "infinite deal of nothing," shut them up and give the gist of their dialogue in a few succinct sentences of your own. Note how in ¶ 10, 11 Hawthorne has condensed the conversation which doubtless occurred at the supper table, and has given us the salient points without the commonplaces that it must have contained:

> He was of a proud yet gentle spirit, haughty and reserved among the rich and great, but ever ready to stoop his head to the lowly cottage door and be like a brother or a son at the poor man's fireside.... He had traveled far and alone; his whole life, indeed, had been a solitary path, for, with the lofty caution of his nature, he had kept himself apart from those who might otherwise have been his companions....
>
> The secret of the young man's character was a high and abstracted ambition. He could have borne to live an undistinguished life, but not to be forgotten in the grave.

and how in ¶ 13 he has given us the trend of the young man's rhapsody, instead of wearying us with what was probably rather a long and tiresome speech:

> There was a continual flow of natural emotion gushing forth amid abstracted reverie which enabled the family to understand this young man's sentiment, though so foreign from their own.

One form of the talkative short story that forms a serious stumbling block to the novice is the dialect story. If you have an idea of trying that style of composition, let me warn you: Don't! Dialect stories never were very artistic, for they are a paradoxical attempt to make good literature of poor rhetoric and worse grammar. They have never been recognized or written by any great master of fiction. They are a sign of a degenerate taste, and their production or perusal is a menace to the formation and preservation of a good literary style. They are merely a fad, which is already of the past; and to-day public and publisher turn in nausea from a mess of dialect which yesterday they would have greedily devoured; so that now there is even no pecuniary excuse for dialect stories. They were doomed to an ephemeral existence, for what little charm they ever possessed was based upon the human craving for something odd and new; the best stories of Barrie and Maclaren live because of their intense human feeling, and they would have succeeded as well and endured longer if they had been clothed in literary English.

"That there is good in dialect none may deny; but that good is only when it chances, as rarely, to be good dialect; when it is used with just discretion and made the effect of circumstances naturally arising, not the cause and origin of the circumstance itself. When the negro, the 'cracker' or the mountaineer dialect occurs naturally in an American story, it often gives telling effects of local color and of shading. But the negro or 'cracker' story *per se* can be made bearable only by the pen of a master; and even then it may be very doubtful if that same pen had not proved keener in portraiture, more just to human nature in the main, had the negro or the 'cracker' been the mere episode, acting on the main theme, and itself reacted on by that."[30]

Study carefully, as models of good character analysis and presentation, Stevenson's "Markheim;" Hawthorne's "The Great Stone Face;" Ichabod Crane in Irving's "The Legend of Sleepy Hollow;" Poe's "William Wilson;" Louisa Ellis in Wilkins' "A New England Nun;" Van Bibber in Davis' "Van Bibber and Others;" Henry St. George in James' "The Lesson of the Master."

FOOTNOTES:

[28] "Rudimentary Suggestions for Beginners in Story Writing," by E. F. Andrews. *Cosmopolitan*. Feb., '97.

[29] "Names in Fiction," by H. H. F. *Literature*. Jan. 19, '99.

[30] "The Day of Dialect," by T. C. De Leon. *Lippincott's*. Nov., '97.

METHODS OF NARRATION

Not only must you have a story to tell, but you must tell it well. The charm and interest of a story come not from the plot itself but from your handling of it. The question of the proper method of narration is to a considerable extent a matter of suitability—of giving the narrative an appropriate setting; it is also a matter of the point of view of the narrator—whether he is to tell the story as one of the actors, or simply as an impersonal observer. A dozen master story writers would tell the same tale in a dozen different ways, and each of them would seem to be the right way; for each writer would view the events from a particular angle, and would make his point of view seem the natural one. But the novice is not always happy in his choice of a view point; or rather, he lacks the knowledge and experience that would teach him how to treat his subject from the particular side from which he has chosen to consider it. Yet a capable and clever writer may sometimes find himself puzzled to choose between a number of methods, any one of which seems appropriate and any one of which he feels himself competent to handle satisfactorily: the question is which one will be for him the most successful method of exploiting his thoughts.

That question should be settled with regard to the suitability of the method to the matter of the story—and here suitability is synonymous with naturalness. It must not be forgotten that story writing is only a modern phase of the world-old custom of story telling, and that the printed page should appear as natural and easy to the eye as the voice would to the ear. When in the twilight the grandmother gathers the children about her knee for a story, whether it be a bit of her own life or a tale from a book, she does not strive after effect, but tells the story simply and naturally, just as she knows it will best suit the children. And so the story writer should tell his tale—so naturally and easily that the reader will forget that he is gazing at the printed page, and will believe himself a spectator at an actual scene in real life.

The great difficulty of the novice is to subordinate his own personality. He knows that he must individualize his story, and that that is best done by putting something of himself into it; and he does not always understand that it is only his spirit that is wanted, and that his body will be very much in the way. Then, too, he is apt to be a little self-conscious, if not actually self-conceited, and he rather likes the idea of putting himself into his work so thoroughly that the reader must always be conscious of his presence. He likes to show his superior knowledge and to take the reader into his confidence; so he indulges in side remarks, and criticisms, and bits of moralizing, and in general exhibits an exasperating tendency to consider himself and his personal opinion of far greater importance than the story which he is expected to tell.

But above all things else the author must keep himself out of sight, and must refrain from interpolating his opinions. He is supposed to be an impersonal person, a human machine through the medium of which the story is preserved, and he has no proper place in his narrative. One no more expects or desires a speech from him than a sermon from a penny-in-the-slot phonograph which has been paid for a comic song. He may stand behind the scenes and manipulate the puppets and speak for them, but his hand must be unseen, his voice carefully disguised, and his personality imperceptible; no one cares for the man who makes the Punch and Judy show—he is judged by the success of his imitation of life, and his own appearance will speedily disillusionize his public. Every time you address your public as "dear reader," "gentle reader,"—or, as Mark Twain has it, "savage reader"—you force upon that public a realization of your presence which is as disagreeable and inartistic as the appearance of the Punch and Judy man, hat in hand, seeking a few coppers in payment of the amusement he has provided.

In the short story no personal confidences, moralizing comments, or confessions are allowed. If you must express your opinions and make your personality felt, write lectures, sermons, essays, books, letters for the public press—but *don't* write short stories. Men read short stories to be amused, not instructed; and they will quickly revolt at any attempt on your part to introduce into your narrative a sugar-coated argument or sermon.

There are certain methods of story telling much affected by the amateur which are particularly difficult to do well. He should especially eschew stories related in the first person, those told by letters, and those in the form of a diary. Notice, I do not say that these methods are absolutely bad: they have been successfully used by masters; but they are at least questionable, and they contain so many pitfalls for the unwary that it is far better for the uninitiated to let them severely alone.

Narrative in the first person gives a certain realism through the mere use of the pronoun "I," and so excites some measure of the desired personal interest; but the same result may be secured, without the accompanying disadvantages, by making the characters do a good deal of talking. That method escapes the danger of getting the narrator between the story and the reader; for the puppet who "I's" his way through the narrative is apt to be rather an important fellow, who intrudes on the most private scenes, and who prefers moralizing and philosophizing to the legitimate furthering of the plot; thus he runs no small risk of making himself unpopular with the reader, and so proving of detriment to the success of the story and of the author.

Then, too, when the author is speaking in his own proper person the reader cannot help wondering at times how one man could know so much about what was going on, even if he were a veritable Paul Pry; while we have become so used to granting the omniscience and omnipresence of the invisible third person author that we never question his knowledge. If, however, the hero-narrator attempt natural modesty and profess to but slight information concerning the story, he is usually a most dull and uninteresting fellow, who is endeavoring to relate a matter of which he has missed the most essential parts. And at all times, though he be a model in all other respects, the very fact that the hero is telling the story lessens its interest, since no matter what harrowing experiences he has suffered, he has come safely through; thus the narrative lacks that anxiety for the hero's welfare which is so large a factor in the delights of fiction.

"It (first person narrative) is better adapted, no doubt, to adventure than to analysis, and better to the expression of humour than to the realization of tragedy. As far as the presentation of *character* is concerned, what it is usual for it to achieve ... is this: a life size, full length, generally too flattering portrait of the hero of the story—a personage who has the limelight all to himself—on whom no inconvenient shadows are ever thrown; ... and then a further graceful idealization, an attractive pastel, you may call it, the lady he most frequently admired, and, of the remainder, two or three Kit-Cat portraits, a head and shoulders here, and there a stray face."[31]

Stories written in the epistolary or diary form suffer all the disadvantages of first person narrative; but they are also liable to others, equally serious, which are peculiarly their own. They are seldom natural, in the first place, for granted that people really do keep interesting diaries or write literary letters, it is rare in either case that a story would be told with technical correctness. And such narratives are usually poor in technique, for their form necessitates the introduction of much that is commonplace or irrelevant, and it also requires the passage of time and causes breaks in the thread of the plot. These forms are favorites with the inexperienced because they seem to dodge some of the difficulties that beset the way of the literary aspirant. Their form is necessarily loose and disjointed, and their style rambling and conversational, and these qualities are characteristic of the work of novices.

"But if fictitious letters are so seldom anything but tiresome, is this because 'the age of letter writing is past?' ... The unpopularity of the epistolary form as a method of authorship is, in fact, due quite as much to a change of taste as to the decay of letter writing. The old practice was of a piece with the unrealities of the eighteenth century, both in art and letters. It necessitated an abundance of superfluous detail, and it was a roundabout, artificial way of doing what the true artist could do much better, simply and directly. It gave, of course, an opportunity of exhibiting subjectively many 'fine shades' of feeling. But it is certainly much more difficult to carry conviction in inventing letters for fictitious persons than in making them converse. In the latter case there is a background; there is the life and movement of the various characters, the spontaneity of question and reply, and the running interchange of talk, all helping to keep a spell upon the reader. The letter gives much less chance of illusion, and we may very soon become conscious of the author—instead of the suffered correspondent—beating his brains for something to say next."[32]

Another poor method, indicative of callowness, is making the hero, so to speak, an animal or a thing, and permitting it to tell its own story. This has peculiar charm for the tyro because of its supposed originality, but it is really as old as story telling itself. It offends greatly against naturalness, for however one may believe in the story of Balaam's ass, or delight in Æsop's talking brutes or Greece's talking statues, one cannot restrain a feeling of skepticism when a dog or a coin is put forward, given human attributes, and made to view the world through man's eyes. On the other hand, if the writer attempts to read the thoughts of the brute or the thing, the difficulty at once presents itself that he can only guess at the mental processes of the one, and that the other is incapable of thought; so that in either case the result is unsatisfactory. One exception to this statement must be made:

Kipling, in his "Jungle Book" stories, seems to have achieved the impossible and read for us the very thoughts of the brute creation. Unfortunately it is not given us to know how nearly he has hit their mental processes; but his animals certainly do not think with the thoughts of men and their cogitations, as he interprets them, appear to us perfectly logical and natural. Yet the success of Kipling does not at all lessen the force of my general statement, for there are few writers who would care to cross pens with him here. Even our own Joel Chandler Harris, in his delightful Uncle Remus stories, has succeeded only in giving his animals human ideas and attributes. The whole endeavor to endow the rest of creation with man's intelligence is too thoroughly artificial to offer a profitable field to the short story writer.

Again, novices err frequently through introducing a multiplicity of narrators, either writing a patchwork story in which all take a hand, or placing narration within narration as in the "Arabian Nights." The method of allowing a number of persons consecutively to carry on the plot is very attractive, since it offers a way of introducing a personally interested narrator without making him preternaturally wise; and it also affords opportunity for the author to exhibit his skill in viewing events from all sides and through the minds of several very different persons. It is, however, open to most of the first person objections, and it is liable to produce a disjointed narrative; but it is particularly unhappy in the short story because it necessitates the introduction and disposition of a number of important people.

The use of narration within narration is more objectionable. It is of little importance who tells the story, or how it came to be told; the less the narrator appears the better. It is seldom that more than one narrator is necessary, yet two, three, or even more are often introduced, with full descriptions of persons and circumstances. "It is a frequent device of the unpractised to cover pages with useless explanations of how they heard a tale which is thus elaborately put too far off from the reader to appeal to his sympathies. One writer, after describing a rural station, his waiting for the train, its appearance when it arrives, the companions of his journey, and so on, is wrecked, and spends the night on a log with an old farmer, who spins him a domestic yarn that has nothing to do with what went before. Why not give the tale direct, in the character of the old farmer? There is no law against that."[33]

This practice is due to the fact that amateurs usually begin by writing strictly true stories, and they always consider it of prime importance that they had the tale from grandmother, or that it actually occurred to John's wife's second cousin's great aunt; forgetting, in their unconscious egotism, that the reader cares only for the narrative, and nothing for the narrator. Stories told to interested listeners by "grandma," an "old hunter," or some loquacious "stranger," usually need to be so revised that the intrusive relater will disappear, merged in the unobtrusive author. Indeed, it is policy so to revise them, for the editor usually considers the author who begins thus too amateurish for him:

"Your turn now, Captain," was the exclamation of several gentlemen who were seated around a table, telling stories, narrating adventures, playing cards and drinking each others' healths.

"What will you have, gentlemen?" inquired Captain R——, a tall, handsome man of middle age, who had been in command of a large ocean steamer many years.

"Oh, one of your adventures," said one of the party; "for surely you must have had some."

"Ah, very well, gentlemen—I remember one that will no doubt interest you; here it is:"

For at the outset he knows, and he knows that his readers will know, that the tale ends thus:

"So ends my story, gentlemen; now let us have a drink to the health of the young sailor's wife, the dearest woman in the world."

"And why not the sailor's health, too?" asked one of the gentlemen.

"All right, sir, just as you please, gentlemen, for I was that sailor."

and that the intervening story is apt to be every whit as stale and conventional as its beginning and its end. Irving's "Tales of a Traveller" show how this method may be used successfully; yet it required all of Irving's art to make the extra-narrative passages readable, and it is an open question if the stories would not have been improved by isolation.

The best method of narration, the simplest and most natural, is to tell the story in the third person, as if you were a passive observer; to make the characters active and conversational; and to permit nothing, not even your own personality, to get between the reader and the story.

FOOTNOTES:

[31] "The Short Story," by Frederick Wedmore. *Nineteenth Century.* Mar., '98.

[32] "The Epistolary Form." *Literature.* Apr. 7, '99.

[33] "Magazine Fiction and How Not to Write It," by Frederick M. Bird. *Lippincott's.* Nov., '94.

VIII

THE BEGINNING

The crucial test of the short story is the manner in which it begins. Of three-fourths of the MSS. submitted to him the editor seldom reads more than the first page, for he has learned by experience that if the story lacks interest there, it will in all probability be lacking throughout. Therefore it behooves you to make the beginning as attractive and correct as possible.

The beginning of a good short story will seldom comprise more than two or three paragraphs, and often it can be compressed into one. If it cannot get to the story proper in that space there is something radically wrong—probably in the plot; for the conventional brevity of the short story requires particular conciseness in the introduction.

In every story there are certain foundation facts that must be understood by the reader at the outset if he would follow the narrative easily. These basic truths differ greatly in different stories, so that it is difficult to give a complete list; but they are usually such details as the time and scene of the story, the names, descriptions, characteristics, and relationships of the different characters, and the relation of events prior to the story that may influence its development. You must make sure that the details which you select are fundamental and that they do have a definite influence which requires some knowledge of them. Any or all of these facts, however, may be introduced later in the narrative when their need appears; or they may be left in abeyance to enhance the element of suspense or mystery.

But because they are necessary these facts need not be listed and ticketed like the *dramatis personae* of a play bill. They should be introduced so deftly that the reader will comprehend them involuntarily; they must seem an intrinsic part of the warp and woof of the narrative. In themselves they are commonplaces, tolerated only because they are necessary; and if they cannot be made interesting they can at least be made unobtrusive. To begin a story thus is to make a false start that may prove fatal:

> This happy family consisted of six; a father, mother, two sons, and two daughters. Clara, the eldest, had completed a course at college, and during the past few months had been completing one in cooking, guided and instructed by her mother. Bessie, the youngest, was five years old. She sat rocking Amanda, her new doll, and was asking her all manner of questions. John and Henry, aged respectively ten and fourteen years, were helping their father.
>
> Grandma and grandpa were expected to dinner; also Mr. Draco, or "Harry," as every one called him. He was a friend of the family's, and Clara's lover.

Note how Hawthorne handles a very similar family group in the initial paragraph of "The Ambitious Guest." He inserts his details without apparent effort; and yet he makes the persons individual and distinct. He does not say:

> This family was happy, and comprised father, mother, grandmother, daughter of seventeen, and younger children.

but:

> The faces of the father and mother had a sober gladness; the children laughed. The eldest daughter was the image of Happiness at seventeen, and the aged grandmother, who was knitting in the warmest place, was the image of Happiness grown old.

Sometimes, in stories which consist largely of conversation, as so many of our modern stories do, the author never directly states the situation to the reader: it is made sufficiently plain either directly in the conversation itself, or indirectly in the necessary comments and descriptions. Or it may be presented as a retrospect indulged in by one of the characters. On the stage this takes the form of a soliloquy; but since few men in their right minds really think aloud, in the short story it is better for the author to imagine such thoughts running through the mind of the character, and to reproduce them as indirect discourse. We are so used to consider the author as omniscient that we experience no surprise or incredulity at such mind-reading. Such stories approach very nearly to the pure *Dramatic Form*. These are at once the most natural and the most artistic methods of introducing essential facts, and they are methods which can be advantageously employed to some extent in almost any story. With this method in mind read carefully any one of Hope's "Dolly Dialogue" stories and note how cleverly the facts are presented through the words and actions of the characters.

In the novel essential details are frequently held in suspense for some time, in order that the opening pages may be made attractive by the introduction of smart conversation or rapid action. A similar method is often followed in the short story, and it cannot be condemned offhand, for if used skillfully it is a clever and legitimate device for immediately fixing the reader's attention; but it holds danger for the uninitiated, for the amateur is liable to postpone the introduction of the details until the story is hopelessly obscure, or until he is reduced to dragging in those essential facts in the baldest manner. Even if he is otherwise successful, he runs the risk of destroying the proportion of his story by practically beginning it in the middle and endeavoring to go both ways at once. The conventions of the short story allow of little space for the retrospection necessary to such an introduction; and when the writer begins to say, "But first let me explain how all this came about," the reader begins to yawn, and the charm of the opening sentences is forgotten in the dreariness of the ensuing explanations. This method is of the modern school of short story writers, but Hawthorne, in "The Prophetic Pictures," gives us an excellent example of how it may be used to advantage; and the following well illustrates the absurd lengths to which it may be carried, and the desperate means to which the writer must then resort to patch up the broken thread of the narrative:

Joseph Johnson was a young man whose name appeared in the list of the dead heroes who had fallen at Santiago.

When Mamie Williams read the startling fact, her eyes filled with tears, as past history was unfolding itself in her mind, presenting one event after another. She thought about their early love, how she had clasped his hand and how his lips lingered long upon hers when last they parted before he started to the cruel war.

With a wounded heart and tear-stained eyes, she sank into a chair, and with her hands over her face, many reflections of the past chased each other through her mind.

She tried to console herself and smooth out the wrinkles in her troubled mind with the thought that God knows and does all things well. She was an intelligent girl, and reasoned farther with herself, "As all hope for Joseph has fled, I ought to marry some one else, and make most of what I have. There is Thomas Malloy, who loves me almost as well; however, my affection for him is not very great, but I think I shall unite my life with his, and do my best to make myself and the world around me happy."

Her mind, moved by an emotion of a noble heart, caused her to make the last remark.

Soon they were married, but there was no happiness in life for her; for the one she lived for was gone, and had carried off her affection with him.

Returning to the war we find that Joseph was not killed in the battle but was taken prisoner by the enemy.

There is a questionable sort of beginning, which might be called dilatory, that consists in carrying the literary aspect of the essential facts to the extreme, and making them occupy a deal more valuable space than is rightly theirs. This is generally the method of a past school of short story writers, or of the writers of to-day who are not yet well versed in the technique of their art. Of this class Washington Irving is a great example. In "Rip Van Winkle" and "The Legend of Sleepy Hollow" he devotes to the introduction almost as much space as a writer to-day would give to the whole tale. He is so skillful in gently urging the narrative along, while he introduces new essentials and interpolates literary but non-essential matter, that in neither story can one exactly fix the bounds of the beginning; but in each a modern story teller would combine the first ten paragraphs into one introductory paragraph. I do not mean to say that this is a fault in Irving: if it is a fault at all it belongs to his time; then, too, these tales were supposed to be written by the garrulous antiquarian, Diedrich Knickerbocker; but their discursive style is not in vogue to-day, and is therefore to be avoided.

As an awful example of the extent to which this dilly-dallying may be carried, let me introduce the following:

> The train rolled onward with a speed of twenty-five miles an hour, the great iron engine puffing and screeching as if its very sides would burst. In the rear car of the six coaches which seemed to follow the monstrous iron horse with dizzy speed, sat an aged man holding a pretty child of four summers, who was fast asleep. The grandfather gazed on the sleeping face and deeply sighed. His thoughts returned to the long ago when his only child was the same age as the little one he held so fondly clasped in his dear old arms. He thought how years ago he had held his own darling thus; how happy and bright his home had been in those sweet bygone days. He recalled how she had been reared in a home of plenty, how she had everything which constitutes the happiness of a young girl.
>
> ### *The Story.*
>
> The time was a warm summer evening in August, the place one of those quiet little towns west of the great Mississippi, and the scene opens in a neat little parlor where a number of young folks had gathered to tender a fitting reception to a newly married couple. A few days previous a stranger had arrived in the town to visit some former friends; these friends attended the reception and were accompanied by their guest. The stranger was formally introduced to the crowd of merry-makers as Elmer Charleston. He was a tall, splendidly formed, intelligent looking young man. Among the young women present was one Jennie Shelby, who was but little more than twenty; she was a blonde, of graceful figure, with a peculiarly animated expression of countenance. Her complexion was beautiful, her dimples deep and mischievous, her large blue eyes full of latent fire, and her features would pass muster among sculptors. Suitors had she by the score. At last she had met her fate. Elmer Charleston accepted a position in the town and at once began to court the only daughter of Squire Shelby.

It seems almost incredible that any writer, however inexperienced, should begin his narrative in this fashion. The introductory paragraph is of course entirely unnecessary—even the author had some inkling of that fact, for he takes pains to specify when "the story" proper actually begins; but even after he is supposed to be in the midst of his narration, he stops to give us wholly gratuitous information concerning the time of day, the state of the weather, and the occasion when Elmer Charleston first met Jennie Shelby—all of which was apparently introduced for the purpose of discouraging further interest: at least, that is what it certainly accomplishes.

The short story has no space for the "glittering generalities" with which young writers delight to preface their work. A tale which requires a page or even a paragraph to elucidate its relation to life and things in general is seldom worth the perusal, much less the writing. These introductory remarks are usually in the nature of a moral, or a bit of philosophizing; but if the story has any point it will be evident in the narrative itself, and no preliminary explanation will atone for later neglect to make it of human interest. There is no good reason, unless it be the perversity of human nature, why you should begin a story by making trite remarks about things in general, as this writer did:

> Love is a very small word, but the feeling that it expresses bears the richest and choicest fruit of any vine that curls its clinging tendrils around the human heart. And a bosom without it is a bosom without warmth; a life without it is like a honeysuckle without its nectar; a heart that has never felt its sweet emotions is like a rosebud that has never unfolded. But in some people it remains latent for a number of years, like an apple which remains green and hard for a time, but suddenly ripens into softness, so when love flashes into the human breast, the once hard heart is changed into mellowness.
>
> Mary Green was just such a character as the one last described, etc.

It would be wrong, however, to say that the prefatory introduction is the sign of a poor story, for many good writers produce such stories, and many critical editors accept and publish them. A large majority of Poe's tales begins so; yet in nearly every case the beginning could have been cut and the story improved. Kipling, too, has a liking for this method of beginning; usually he states his abstract idea, as a preacher announces his text, and then proceeds to make the practical application. With these masters the transition from the general to the specific is usually easy and gradual, but in the following example from Kipling's "On the Strength of a Likeness" the line of demarcation is well defined:

> Next to a requited attachment, one of the most convenient things that a young man can carry about with him at the beginning of his career is an unrequited attachment. It makes him feel important and business-like, and *blasé*, and cynical; and whenever he has a touch of liver, or suffers from want of exercise, he can mourn over his lost love, and be very happy in a tender, twilight fashion.

> Hannasyde's affair of the heart had been a godsend to him. It was four years old, etc.

There is no real abruptness here, and the author's observations are apt and sound; but the fact remains that they are not essential and so a strict observance of conventions requires their elimination.

"The background of a story should always be the last thing to be chosen, but it is the first thing to consider when one comes to actual writing out. A story is much like a painting.... In story writing it appears to be simple portraits that need least background."[34] Scenes may play an important part in a story by influencing the actors or by offering a contrast to the events; in such cases they must be made specific, but rather after the broad free manner of the impressionist. The employment of the contrast or harmony of man and nature is one of the oldest devices of story telling, but also one of the most artistic and effective. It is not an artificial device, though it occasionally appears so from its misuse: it is a fact that all of us must have experienced in some degree, for we are all, though often unconsciously, influenced by the weather or by our environments; and though our emotions may be so intense as to counteract that influence, we are sufficiently self-centered to think it strange that all nature should not be in harmony with us.

You should, however, take care that the scene is important before you attempt to present it. Unless it does influence the action of the story or is necessary for the understanding of what is to come it has no place in the narrative, no matter how great may be its beauties or how artistic your description of them. Above all things, never clutter your story with commonplaces and details which would serve to picture any one of a hundred different places. "When a tale begins, 'The golden orb of day was slowly sinking among the hills, shedding an effulgent glory over the distant landscape,' the discerning reader, whether official or volunteer, is apt to pause right there. He knows exactly what happens when the orb of day finds it time to disappear, and he does not care for your fine language unless it conveys a fact or an idea worth noting."[35]

The best method of procedure is to suggest the scene, as you do the character,[36] by the few specific features which distinguish it from other similar scenes, and to permit the reader's imagination to fill in the details. Hawthorne gives a very distinct idea of the setting of "The Ambitious Guest;" and yet, from his description alone, no two persons would draw the same picture. It suffices that they would all possess the essential elements of loneliness, bleakness and haunting terror. At the same time he effects a sharp contrast between the wildness and discomforts of the night and the peace and cheer of the tavern.

In locating the story it is absurdly shiftless to designate the place by a dash or a single letter, or a combination of the two. One of your first objects is to make your story vivid, and you will not further that end by the use of impossible or indefinite substitutes for names. If you are relating a true story and desire to disguise it, adopt or invent some appellation different enough to avoid detection; but never be so foolish as to say:

> The story I am about to relate occurred to my friend X., in the little village of Z——, during the latter part of the year 18—.

It would be just as sensible to go through the rest of the story and substitute blanks or hieroglyphics for the important words. Specificness in minor details is a great aid to vividness, and you cannot afford to miss that desirable quality through sheer laziness.

The safest way to begin a story is to begin at the beginning, state the necessary facts as succinctly as possible, and lead the reader into the quick of the action before he has had time to become weary. For it must be remembered that the object of the short story is always to amuse, and that even in the introductory paragraphs the reader must be interested. If he is not he will very likely cast the story aside as dry and dull; if he does read it through he will be prejudiced at the outset, so that the result will be about the same.

In "The Ambitious Guest" the introduction occupies ¶ 1-4, or one-eleventh of the entire story, measured by paragraphs. In that space Hawthorne locates the scene, introduces and individualizes the characters, determines the atmosphere of the tale, and recounts the necessary preliminaries; and all this he does in the easiest way, while skillfully leading up to the story proper. A writer of to-day would probably condense these four paragraphs into one, without neglecting any essentials; but he would hardly attain the literary finish of Hawthorne's work.

To prove further that the beginning of a story does influence its success, I would ask you to consider the following, which is typical of the style of introduction most affected by the novice:

It was a bright, crisp, twilight evening, and two young girls sat together in a richly furnished parlor of a splendid country house.

One, tall and slender, with a richly moulded figure; handsome brunette features, and raven tresses—Edith Laingsford, the daughter of the house; the other, a girl of medium height, with a figure perfectly rounded, and a fair Grecian face.

Her eyes were of a soft gray, and her hair a waving chestnut. She was Marion Leland, a dependent cousin of Miss Laingsford's.

Now, frankly, do you care to read further? Surely there is nothing in the glimpse of the plot here presented that encourages you to hope that the tale may improve upon further perusal. From these three paragraphs you can construct the whole story: you know that the "dependent cousin" and the girl with the "handsome brunette features" will be rivals for the affections of some "nice young man" of corresponding conventionality, and that the poor relation will finally win him—chiefly because it always happens so in stories and seldom in real life. And you know from these specimen paragraphs that there will be nothing in the handling of this poor old hackneyed plot that will repay its perusal. Of course there is always a chance that you may be mistaken in your surmises; but the chance is too slight, and you cast the story aside with a yawn, even as the editor would do. See to it, then, that your own stories do not deserve like treatment.

FOOTNOTES:

[34] "How to Write Fiction." Published anonymously by Bellaires & Co., London. Part I, Chapter VII.

[35] "Magazine Fiction and How Not to Write It," by Frederick M. Bird. *Lippincott's.* Nov., '94.

[36] See Chapter VI.

THE STORY PROPER

The correct short story possesses unity of form as well as unity of plot. In the novel there may be wide gaps of time and scene between adjacent chapters; but the short story allows of no such chasms of thought, much less of chapters. Parts or chapters in a short story are uncanonical. A short story is essentially a unit, and the necessity of divisions indicates the use of a plot that belongs to some larger form of literature; but the indicated "parts" or "chapters" may be false divisions introduced through the influence of the conventions of the novel.

The various divisional signs to be avoided are the separate entries or letters of the diary or epistolary forms, the introduction of stars or blank spaces to indicate a hiatus, and the division of the narrative into parts or chapters. The evils of the diary and epistolary forms have already been discussed and need no further comment. The use of stars or spaces either is due to an improper plot, or is entirely unnecessary. In the first instance the fault is radical, and the only remedy is complete reconstruction; in the second case the difficulty resolves itself into an ignorance or a disregard of rhetorical conventions. Often the story is deliberately divided and forced to appear in several chapters when its plot and treatment make its unity very evident; and solely because the amateur has an idea, caught from his novel reading, that such divisions are essential to a well told story. They are not necessary to many novels, though they may be convenient; and they have no place in the scheme of the short story. There are stories, "short" at least in length, in which divisions are necessary to indicate breaks which do not seriously interrupt the coherency of the narrative; they may be readable stories, but they can never be models.

The ideal short story, from the point of unity, is one which requires the passage of the least time and presents the fewest separate incidents. It is the relation of a single isolated incident, which occupies only the time required to tell it. "The Ambitious Guest" impresses the reader as a single incident and would seem to approach this perfection, but a careful analysis of it resolves it into a number of minor incidents, so closely related and connected that at first glance they appear to form a perfect whole. The component incidents of the body of "The Ambitious Guest" (¶ 5-39) are:

¶ 5-7. The stranger praises the fire and reveals his destination.

¶ 8, 9. A stone rolls down the mountain side. (Lapse of time indicated here.)

¶ 10, 11. The characters are described, as they reveal themselves through their conversation.

¶ 12-23. They converse rather frankly of their several ambitions.

¶ 24-27. A wagon stops before the inn, but goes on when the landlord does not immediately appear.

¶ 28-31. A touch of sentimental byplay between the stranger and the maid.

¶ 32. A sadness creeps over the company, caused, perhaps, by the wind wailing without.

¶ 33-39. The grandmother discusses her death and burial.

None of these incidents, except those containing the rolling stone and the passing travelers, possess sufficient action or identity to be called an incident, except for some such analytical purpose. They are rather changes in the subject under discussion than separate happenings. With the exception already noted, it may be said that there is no time gap between these incidents, for each one begins at the expiration of its predecessor. The connection and relation of the sub-incidents is not always as close as this. In a longer story they could be more distinct and definite and yet preserve the unity of the work; but they should never disintegrate into minor climaxes,[37] nor into such a jerky succession of disassociated scenes as the following:

On a fair sweet spring morning in the lovely month of May, Squire Darley finishes an important letter. He reads it over the second time to see that there is no mistake.

"There, that'll do, I think," he soliloquizes. "And that'll fetch him, I think. Peculiar diseases require peculiar remedies." And he chuckled to himself. Then with deliberate care he addressed it to "Mr. H. C. Darley, New York City."

A few words to my reader, and we will then follow this important letter. Five years before the time of which we write, Abner Vanclief, a poor but honorable gentleman, had died, leaving his motherless daughter to the sole care of his lifelong friend, Horace Darley, a wealthy country gentleman, a widower, with only one son.

Squire Darley was quite at a loss to know what to do with this, his new charge. He did not think it fit and proper to take her to Darley Dale, with only himself and servants as companions. Then, too, she was sadly in need of schooling.

At last after much worry on his part, it was satisfactorily arranged between himself and a maiden sister, that resided in Albany, that Violet was to remain with her, attend the best college, pay strict attention to her studies and music, and when her education should be completed, she, if she wished, was to make Darley Dale her future home.

Four years passed swiftly by, and then "Dear Aunt Molly," as Violet had learned to call her, was taken violently ill; and before her brother came her sweet spirit had flown away and poor Violet was again alone. But after she became fairly installed as mistress at Darley Dale, she soon learned to love the place and also to love the dear old man that had been to her so staunch a friend.

As for his son Harley, she had heard his praises sung from morning until night. She had never seen him, for at the time of her father's death he was attending college, and before she returned to Darley Dale he had hied himself off to New York City, there to open a law office and declare that his future home.

Many times the Squire had written him beseeching him to return, but always met with a courteous refusal.

When Violet had been at Darley Dale a year she was surprised beyond measure by an offer of marriage from Squire Darley.

He had enlarged upon the fact that his son was a most obstinate young man, that he himself was growing old, and that he wished to see her well cared for before he died.

She had assured him that she could work, and that she was willing to work when the time came, but the old Squire proved himself to be as obstinate as his wilful son. And at last Violet, with a white drawn face, and dark frightened eyes, consented to become his wife at some future time.

And the letter addressed to Mr. H. C. Darley contained the announcement of the engagement of Squire Horace to Miss Violet Vanclief.

It is seldom that even a model short story plot will be a perfect unit, for in the story, as in the life which it pictures, some slight change of scene and some little passage of time are inevitable. Thus in any short story there is usually a slight hiatus of thought, due to these causes, which must be bridged over. The tyro will span the chasm by means of stars or some such arbitrary signs, but the master will calmly ignore such gaps and preserve the unity of his narrative so deftly that even the lines of the dovetailing will be scarcely visible. Thus in "The Ambitious Guest" (¶ 9, 10) Hawthorne had need to indicate the passage of some little time, during which the guest had his supper; but the breach is passed in so matter-of-fact a manner that there is no jolt, and yet the sense of time is secured:

> Let us now suppose the stranger to have finished his supper of bear's meat, and by his natural felicity of manner to have placed himself on a footing of kindness with the whole family; so that they talked as freely together as if he belonged to their mountain-brood.

When the plot comprises a series of closely related episodes the story should be located in the time of the most important one, and all necessary preliminary matter should be introduced as briefly and casually as possible in one of the several ways already given.[38] Indeed, the whole difficulty is usually due to a poor beginning, and properly belongs to the preceding chapter.

Next to the use of divisions comes the error, also caught from the novel, of making the short story a carryall for divers bits of wisdom, moralizing, description, and literary small talk, which have no part in the narrative, but which the clever and self-appreciative author has not the heart to withhold from the public. The art of omission is an important branch of the art of authorship. It is seldom necessary to tell the novice what to put in; but it is frequently necessary to tell him—and oh! so hard to persuade him!—that to introduce an irrelevant idea is worse than to omit a necessary detail. The young writer must learn early and learn once for all the absolute necessity for the exclusion of non-essentials. Selection of details plays an important part in any literary work, but in the short story extreme care is indispensable, for the short story has too little space to sacrifice any to pretty but useless phrases. Such irrelevant matter is usually called "padding," and its presence is a serious detriment to the success of any story, however clever in conception.

One of the chief causes of padding is the desire for "local color"—a term by which we characterize those details which are introduced to make a story seem to smack of the soil. These details must be eminently local and characteristic—possible of application to only the small community to which they are ascribed—or they are mere padding. The need of local color depends much upon the character of the story: it varies from a doubtful addition to the story of ingenuity or adventure, to a necessary part of the story portraying human life and character. "Without blindly indulging in local color one must be accurate in indicating facts. A work of art must not be crowded with so-called local color, but certain facts must be known and used to give the effect of a true relation.... The atmosphere, the feeling and idiosyncrasy—a word or a phrase which reveals character—are the only true local color, not passing phrases of unkempt speech."[39] The stories of Miss Wilkins, Octave Thanet, Bret Harte, and Joel Chandler Harris are full of excellent examples of local color.

Every perfect short story will contain a strong argument for good, through its subtle exposition of the earning of the "wages of sin," but any attempt to make it a medium for the spreading of ethical and spiritual truths will entail ridicule upon the writer and failure upon his work. The only legitimate purpose of the short story is to amuse, and didacticism in literature is always inartistic. "Novels with a purpose" may find publishers and readers; but no one, except the author, cares for "polemic stories—such as set forth the wickedness of Free Trade or of Protection, the Wrongs of Labor and the Rights of Capital, the advantages of one sect over another, the beauties of Deism, Agnosticism, and other unestablished tenets.... Genius will triumph over most obstacles, and art can sugar-coat an unwelcome pill; but in nineteen cases out of twenty the story which covers an apology for one doctrine or an attack upon the other has no more chance than if it were made up of offensive personalities."[40] "Though ordinary dramatic short stories do not have a moral which shows itself, still under the surface in every story is something which corresponds to the moral, and which we shall call *the soul of the story*."[41] The short story cannot properly be a mere sermon, such as are so often penned under the caption of "The Drunkard's Wife," "The Orphan's Prayer," "The Wages of Sin," and other similar titles. It must teach its moral lesson in its own way—its artistic presentation of the great contrast between the sort of men who work deeds of nobility and of shame. If it be saddled with didacticism or tailed with a moral, it ceases to be a story and becomes an argument; when it no longer concerns us.

Indirectly, and perhaps unintentionally, the short story is a great factor for good. The world is weary of the bald sermons of the Puritans, and of their endeavor to "point a tale" by every ordinary occurrence; it is rather inclined to a Pharisaical self-righteousness; and needs to have its sins, and the practical benefits of goodness, cunningly insinuated; but it can never fail to admire and strive to emulate the noble deeds of noble men, whether creatures of flesh or phantoms of the brain. To be sure, many of our best short stories deal with events so slight and really unimportant that they might be said to have no moral influence; yet, if they simply provide us with innocent amusement for an idle hour, their ethical value must not be overlooked; and when they do involve some great moral question or soul crisis their influence is invariably on the right side.

The point is that religion is not literature. The mere fact that the heroine of a story is a poor milk and water creature, full of bald platitudes and conventional righteousness, does not make that narrative correct or readable; indeed, it is very apt to make it neither, for the platitudes will be irrelevant and the righteousness uninteresting. When this old world of ours becomes really moral we may be content to read so-called stories in which goody-good characters parade their own virtues and interlard their ordinary speech with prayers and hymns and scriptural quotations; but while a tithe of the present sin and crime exists our fiction will reflect them with the other phases of our daily life.

Now by this I do not at all mean that religion has no place in literature. Such a ruling would not only be contrary to the practice of our best writers, but would also deprive us of a recognized and important element in human life. The religious influence is one of the most powerful to which man is subject, and as it plays so great a part in our lives it must necessarily figure largely in our stories. But it must be treated there because of the manner in which it influences human life and action, and not from the ethical standpoint: it must be made literature and not religious dogmatism. That it can be so treated and yet retain the full strength of its power for good is best illustrated in the works of Miss Wilkins. Nearly every one of her stories possesses a strong element of New England Puritanism, but there is no attempt to preach or moralize.

The short story must be well proportioned: those parts which are essential differ materially in their importance, and they must be valued and handled in accordance with their influence upon the plot. No scene, however cleverly done, must be allowed to monopolize the space of the story, except in so far as it is necessary to an understanding of what follows; and no incident which furthers the plot, however trivial or ordinary it may seem to you, must be slighted. The preservation of the balance of the story is not wholly a matter of the number of words involved: often a page of idle chatter by the characters makes less impression on the reader than a single terse direct sentence by the author himself; but in general the practice is to value the various parts of the story by the word space accorded them. This rule will not, however, hold good in the case of the climax, which is estimated both by its position and by the manner in which it is worked up to.

The story proper is really only the preparation for the climax. Most stories depend for their interest upon the pleasure with which we follow the principal characters through various trying episodes, and the great desire which we all experience to know "how it all comes out." It is this innate sense, which seems to be a phase of curiosity, that affords the pleasure that the average reader derives from fiction. One seldom stops to consider how a story is written, but judges it by its power to keep him absorbed in the fortunes of its hero and heroine. This is the element of suspense.

However, there finally comes a point when the suspense cannot be longer continued, and the strained attention of the reader is on the verge of collapsing into indifference, when the curiosity must be gratified by at least a partial revelation; and so the element of surprise enters. Too long a strain on the interest is invariably fatal, and the thing is to know when to relieve the tension. Just when this relief should occur depends upon the plot and the length of the story, so that the question must be settled separately for each particular case. As has already been said, the plot of a short story should not be involved; yet it may be permitted some degree of complexity. In such a case it is probable that there must be some preliminary relief of suspense before the final relief which the climax offers. However, because of the usual simplicity of the plot, the length of the story has greater influence in regulating the relief of the suspense. In a story of 3,000 words or less there is neither room nor necessity for any preliminary surprise, and the most effective method is to withhold all hints at the outcome until the actual climax, as Hawthorne did in "The Ambitious Guest." But when the story approaches or exceeds 10,000 words it is probable that there must be some lessening of the tension previous to the climax, as in Henry James' "The Lesson of the Master." This story, which contains 25,000 words, is divided into six parts, each representing a separate scene in the progress of the story; and yet, so skillful is James, there is no hiatus between the parts, and the story as a whole has unity of impression. At the end of each part the reader has made a definite advance toward the point of the story, through the preliminary relief of suspense afforded by that part, as a study of this brief outline will show:

I

At the end Paul Overt first sees Henry St. George, and the reader receives a definite picture of the great author, who has hitherto been only a name.

II

At the end the two meet, and the picture is given life.

III

All through this division St. George reveals to Overt his real character, so that when the end comes Overt has a less exalted idea of the master than that which he had cherished.

IV

At the end Marion Fancourt tells Overt of St. George's declared intention to cease visiting her. This relieves suspense by making Overt's position toward her more definite, but also involves matters because of St. George's failure to give any good reason for his action.

V

At the end Overt, by the advice of St. George, sacrifices in the cause of true art all his natural desires for love and domestic joys.

VI

In the first part Overt learns of St. George's engagement to Miss Fancourt.

At the end St. George tells Overt that he has given up writing to enjoy those very things which he advised Overt to renounce.

A study of this outline will show you the necessity, in the case of this story, of these preliminary reliefs of the suspense. It would have been absurdly impossible to have tried to hold in abeyance until the climax all these matters; nor does the solving of any of these minor perplexities at all lessen the interest in the denouement. Each bit of information comes out at the proper time as a matter of course, just as it would come to our knowledge if we were observing a similar drama in real life.

When the outcome of the writer's meanderings is finally revealed, it should be a veritable surprise—*i. e.*, be unexpected. This is a matter that is rather easily managed, for it is a poor plot that does not afford at least two settlements—either the heroine marries the hero, or she marries the villain; and often there is a third possibility, that she marries neither. If he has provided a proper plot, the author has but little to do with making the surprise genuine, and that little is rather negative. He opens the possibility of the hero doing any one of a number of things, and he may even give rather broad hints, but he should take care never to give a clue to the outcome of the story, unless he purposely gives a misleading clue. The most artistic method is to make these hints progressive and culminative, so that though each one adds to the knowledge of the reader, it is only when they all culminate in the climax that the mystery is completely solved.

This preparation for the climax is one of the most delicate tasks required of the short story writer. The climax must seem the logical result of events and personal characteristics already recited. If it is too startling or unexpected it will be a strain on the credulity of the reader, and will be dubbed "unnatural;" for though fiction allows great license in the employment of strange people and situations, it demands that they be used with some regard for plausibility. The ending must appear inevitable—but its inevitableness must not be apparent until the end has come. It is only after the story has been read that the reader should be able to look back through the narrative and pick out the preparatory touches. They must have influenced him when first he read them and prepared him for what was to come, but without his being conscious of their influence.

The novice usually prepares the way for his climax so carefully that he gives it away long before he should. This he does either by means of anticipatory side remarks, or by making the outcome of his story so obvious at the start that he really has no story to tell, and a climax or surprise is impossible. The first fault is much the easier to correct: most of the side remarks can be cut out bodily without injury to the story, and those which are really necessary can be so modified and slurred over that they will prepare the way for the climax without revealing it. The other fault is usually radical: it is the result of a conventional plot treated in the conventional manner. It is beyond help so far as concerns that particular story, for it requires a new plot handled in an original manner; but its recurrence can be prevented if the writer will be more exacting in his selection of plots, and more individual in his methods. It can usually be detected in the beginning, as in the case of the last example quoted in Chapter VIII.

In "The Ambitious Guest" the climax is led up to most skillfully by Hawthorne; indeed, his preparation is so clever that it is not always easy to trace. Throughout the story there are an air of gloom and a strange turning to thoughts of death that seem to portend a catastrophe; and I believe the following passages are intentional notes of warning:

1 ... a cold spot and a dangerous one.... stones would often rumble down its sides and startle them at midnight.

2 ... the wind came through the Notch and seemed to pause before their cottage, ... wailing and lamentation.... For a moment it saddened them, though there was nothing unusual in the tones.

3 ... whose fate was linked with theirs.

8 (Entire.)

9 (Entire.)

10 ... a prophetic sympathy ... the kindred of a common fate....

12 (Entire.)

14 "... a noble pedestal for a man's statue." (Doubtful.)

16 "... things that are pretty certain never to come to pass."

17 "... when he is a widower."

18 "When I think of your death, Esther, I think of mine too. But I was wishing we had a good farm ... round the White Mountains, but not where they could tumble on our heads ... I might die happy enough in my bed.... A slate gravestone would suit me as well as a marble one...."

20 "They say it's a sign of something when folk's minds go a-wandering so."

22 "... go and take a drink out of the basin of the Flume." (Doubtful; unless regarded as the result of some subtle warning to fly the spot.)

26 ... though their music and mirth came back drearily from the heart of the mountain.

28 ... a light cloud passed over the daughter's spirit....

32 ... it might blossom in Paradise, since it could not be matured on earth ... the wind through the Notch took a deeper and drearier sound.... There was a wail along the road as if a funeral were passing.

36 (Entire.)

38 (Entire.)

39 (Entire.)

A novice writing the same story would hardly have refrained from introducing some very bald hints concerning the fate of the ambitious stranger; for the novice has a mistaken idea that wordy and flowery exclamations make sad events all the sadder, forgetting that silent grief is the keenest. Thus the novice would have interlarded his narrative with such exclamations as:

¶ 12.

Ah! could the unfortunate stranger but have guessed the culmination of his bright dreams, how would he have bewailed his fate!

¶ 19.

Unhappy youth! *his* grave was to be unmarked, his very death in doubt!

¶ 28.

Poor girl! had she a premonition of her awful death?

Such interpolations are very exasperating to the reader, for he much prefers to learn for himself the outcome of the tale; and they also greatly offend against the rhetorical correctness of the story, for they are always utterly irrelevant and obstructive.

The only stories which may properly anticipate their own denouements are what might be called "stories of premonition," in which the interest depends upon comparing actual events to the prophecy of dreams or some other mystical agency. In such tales the real interest is usually in the weirdness of the whole affair—though, to be sure, they do not always turn out as they are expected to. For, after all, this introduction of surprise into fiction is simply an imitation of nature, and "it is the unexpected that always happens."

FOOTNOTES:

[37] See Chapter X.

[38] See Chapter VIII for the best methods of introducing foundation facts.

[39] "The Art of Fiction." A lecture by Gilbert Parker. *The Critic*. Dec., '98.

[40] "Magazine Fiction and How Not to Write It," by Frederick M. Bird. *Lippincott's*. Nov., '94.

[41] "How to Write Fiction." Published anonymously by Bellaires & Co., London. Part I, Chapter V.

CLIMAX AND CONCLUSION

If the overworked editor, hastily skimming the heap of MSS. before him, comes upon one which promises well in the opening paragraphs, he will turn to its conclusion, to learn how well the author has kept his promise; and if he finds there equal evidence of a good story, he will put the MS. by for more careful reading and possible purchase. Experience has taught him that the end of a story is second only to the beginning as a practical test of the narrative; and therefore to the author as well the conclusion is of extreme importance.

The end of a short story comprises the climax and the conclusion. The climax is the chief surprise, the relief of the suspense, or the greatest relief, if there is more than one; it is the apex of interest and emotion; it is the point of the story; it is really *the* story. The conclusion is the solving of all problems, the termination of the narrative itself, and the artistic severing of all relations between narrator and reader.

The climax, in spite of its importance, is but a small part of the story, so far as mere words are concerned. In a properly constructed narrative its influence is felt throughout the whole story, which, as already stated, is but one long preparation for it. But in itself the climax is usually confined to a single paragraph of ordinary length; and the climax proper, the real point of the story, is usually conveyed in a half dozen words. For the climax, and particularly the climax proper, is the story concentrated in a single phrase. It must have been prepared for carefully and worked up to at some length; but when it does come it must be expressed so directly and so forcefully that it will make the reader jump mentally, if not physically. It is the desire to produce this startling effect that leads some writers to endeavor to gain artificial force by printing their climax proper in italics, or even in capitals. In "The Ambitious Guest" we have an unusually strong and perfect climax in ¶ 40, 41:

> ... a sound abroad in the night, rising like the roar of a blast, had grown broad, deep and terrible before the fated group were conscious of it. The house and all within it trembled; the foundations of the earth seemed to be shaken, as if this awful sound was the peal of the last trump. Young and old exchanged one wild glance and remained an instant pale, affrighted, without utterance or power to move. Then the same shriek burst simultaneously from all their lips:

> "The slide! The slide!"

while the climax proper—the climax of the climax—occurs in the four words which compose ¶ 41.

> "The slide! The slide!"

It is hardly necessary to say that the climax should be very near the end of the story, for even those stories which attempt to begin in the middle and go both ways at once place the climax properly. But there is a danger that the climax will come too soon. After they have reached what is properly a central point in their story, amateurs often become lazy or in too great a hurry, and rush the latter part of the narrative through unceremoniously. In the first part they may have been inclined to go into needless detail; but when once they come in sight of the finish, they forget everything except that their task is nearly ended; they plunge ahead regardless, treat important matters most superficially, neglect those skillful little touches which go to make a story natural and literary, and reach the end to find that they have skeletonized an important part of the narrative. In such a case the reader is very apt to come upon the climax unexpectedly, and so to find it forced and illogical; whereas if the author had preserved the proportions of his narrative, and led up to his climax properly, it would have been accounted strong and inevitable.

The climax of a story must be a genuine climax—that is, it must be the culmination of the interest of the story, and it must definitely end and eliminate the element of suspense. The climax, or its immediate consequences, must decide the destinies of all your characters, and the fate of all their schemes. If the heroine is hesitating between her two lovers she must decide in the climax or on account of it; if the hero is in a position of great danger he must be killed or saved. The revelation need not be couched in the bald phrase, "And so John married Kate;" but it may be hinted at or suggested in the most subtle manner; but settled in some way it must be. Stockton did otherwise in "The Lady, or the Tiger?" but he sought for humorous effect, and all things are fair in the funny story. Stories which are meant to be serious, but which leave the reader still puzzling over the possibilities of the plot, are likely to get their author into serious difficulties with the reading public, even if the editors can be persuaded to overlook his idiosyncracies.

The amateur is prone to the conviction, deduced, I fear, from the practice of the cheap melodrama and the cheaper novel, that "climax" and "tragedy" are synonymous terms, and that he is violating sacred traditions unless he ends his tale with a violent death. But it is by no means necessary that the climax of a short story should be or should contain a catastrophe or a tragedy. Its nature depends entirely upon the character of the tale in which it appears, and it may be just as strong and just as thrilling if it consists only of the "Yes" with which the heroine answers the hero's wooing. Indeed, it not infrequently happens that the tragedy or the catastrophe which appears in the climax is only an accessory to the real climax, a cause or a result of it. The climax of "The Ambitious Guest" is a tragedy; but the climax of Irving's "The Legend of Sleepy Hollow," though certainly a catastrophe, is anything but tragic, if read in the ironic spirit in which it was written:

> Another convulsive kick in the ribs, and old Gunpowder sprang upon the bridge; he thundered over the resounding planks; he gained the opposite side; and now Ichabod cast a look behind to see if his pursuer should vanish, according to rule, in a flash of

fire and brimstone. Just then he saw the goblin rising in his stirrups, and in the very act of hurling his head at him. Ichabod endeavored to dodge the horrible missile, but too late. It encountered his cranium with a tremendous crash; he was tumbled headlong into the dust, and Gunpowder, the black steed, and the goblin rider passed by like a whirlwind.

While in Poe's "The Black Cat," one tragedy is a preliminary of the climax and another is in a manner the result of it; but the real climax is the discovery of the cat:

> ... a dozen stout arms were toiling at the wall. It fell bodily. The corpse, already greatly decayed and clotted with gore, stood erect before the eyes of the spectators. On its head, with red extended mouth and solitary eye of fire, sat the hideous beast whose craft had seduced me into murder, and whose informing voice had consigned me to the hangman. I had walled the monster up within the tomb!

Nor does the mere introduction of a tragedy make a climax, for though the following paragraphs contain two tragedies, there is no climactic force:

> Joseph, who had been sitting with his head on his knees, and wondering what in the world was going to happen, raised his head, and exclaimed, on seeing his brother, "You have come after me—" At this instant some one struck him on the head with a pistol, which brought him to the floor. But Harry, hearing the familiar voice, and seeing the man also, knew too well who it was. He shouted at the top of his voice, "Stop! Wait! This thing must be investigated!" Telling them who the prisoner was, and pleading with them, he was finally able to disperse the mob, though against their own will.
>
> The next morning, when Mamie was brought to consciousness again, she begged that he should not be punished.
>
> On learning the truth he was immediately released, but the bitter grief, mingled with so much excitement, was more than he could endure. He died that night at ten.
>
> The bitterness occasioned by this catastrophe remained in the bosom of Mamie, and she too died of a broken heart.

The plot of a certain type of story requires subordinate and preliminary climaxes to relieve the tension or advance the action, as already stated.[42] Such periods, when given genuine climactic force, are antagonistic to the spirit of the short story, in that they violate the unity, and a story containing them is usually faulty otherwise; but such stories have been written by good writers and so must be recognized here. The preliminary climaxes must be sufficiently few, sufficiently subordinate and sufficiently distant not to detract from the force of the chief climax. The main point is to see that one of the preliminary climaxes is not really *the* climax, for inexperienced writers sometimes allow their stories to run on longer than they should; or they confuse what is merely an incident with what should be made the main crisis. In "The Ambitious Guest" there is only one climax; but in Hawthorne's "Mr. Higginbotham's Catastrophe" I find no less than five critical points, which I here subpend with the numbers of the paragraphs in which they occur:

¶ 7.

"Old Mr. Higginbotham of Kimballton was murdered in his orchard at eight o'clock last night by an Irishman and a nigger. They strung him up to the branch of a St. Michael's pear tree where nobody would find him till the morning."

¶ 14.

"... if squire Higginbotham was murdered night before last I drank a glass of bitters with his ghost this morning. Being a neighbor of mine, he called me into his store as I was riding by, and treated me...."

¶ 21.

"No, no! There was no colored man. It was an Irishman that hanged him last night at eight o'clock; I came away at seven."

¶ 36.

"I left Kimballton this morning to spend the vacation of commencement-week with a friend about five miles from Parker's Falls. My generous uncle, when he heard me on the stairs, called me to his bedside and gave me two dollars and fifty cents to pay my stage-fare, and another dollar for my extra expenses."

¶ 49.

He rushed forward, prostrated a sturdy Irishman with the butt-end of his whip, and found—not, indeed, hanging on the St. Michael's pear tree, but trembling beneath it with a halter round his neck—the old identical Mr. Higginbotham.

These several climaxes form a perfect series, each a little higher than its predecessor, and all logically culminating in the chief climax of the story in ¶ 49; and by this progressive and culminative effect they go far to preserve the sense of unity which their presence endangers. Such real if minor climaxes are entirely different from the several stages of the story illustrated in Chapter IX by James' "The Lesson of the Master."

The novice usually has some hazy conception of the importance of a climax, and endeavors according to his lights to attain the desired effect, but he is seldom successful. Most frequently he is handicapped by his plot, which is not designed to produce a successful climax. If he has escaped that danger he is liable to ruin a possible good climax by too abrupt an introduction. His nearest approach to success is what may be called a "false" or "technical" climax, in the use of which he is very skillful—too skillful, indeed, for his own good. This false climax is produced by breaking off the narrative abruptly the moment the suspense of the story is terminated. It is really an abrupt conclusion, and not a climax at all; and it produces the jump in the reader's mind by its suddenness, and not by its concentrated force. It is sometimes made more pointed by the use of italics or capitals. Thus the following final paragraphs, which are typical of the work of the novice, have no hint of a climax as they stand:

... Mrs. Moore sat gazing into the glowing grate.

"Well, truants, where have you been all this time? I—" She stopped suddenly as she saw Nettie's blushes, and the happy look on Guy's face.

"Mother, Nettie has made me the happiest man in existence, by consenting to be my wife. And we have come to ask your blessing."

"It is heartily given, my dear children. Nothing could give me more pleasure than to see you two happily married," said she, kissing them. "By the way, how did you young people happen to make this wonderful discovery?"

"Well, mother, I have had some serious thoughts about the matter ever since I surprised you and Nettie last September, but I never dared to put my thoughts into words till to-day."

"I don't remember that you surprised Nettie. She was out in the orchard, she told me, when you arrived."

"Yes, I believe I remember finding her in the orchard," and he gave a ludicrous description of their first meeting.

"That accounts for Nettie's blushes when I introduced you that day. You won't go west now, will you, Guy?"

"I shall have to, mother; but I'll sell out at the first opportunity. In the meantime I think we had better notify aunt Adams that she is doomed to have a son-in-law."

"I have thought of an excellent plan," said Nettie. "Let's all go east for the holidays. Only, for goodness' sake, don't tell Edith and Maud about my exploits in the apple tree. They would be so shocked at my lack of dignity."

So the following week they started for Nettie's home. Guy soon won Mrs. Adams' consent to her daughter's marriage, which was arranged to take place the following September.

"That is the month in which the old apple tree bears its most delicious fruit," Guy whispered to Nettie.

If, however, the author had stopped with the third paragraph, he would have had at least a false or technical climax. This false climax must not be confused with the coincident real climax and abrupt ending discussed further on.

When the climax has come the story has reached its end and the quicker you terminate it the better your reader will be pleased. With the passing of the climax interest ceases, and you have only to gather up and explain the few unsettled points, and round off your narrative gracefully. Any further interest in your characters is little more than a sense of politeness due to old acquaintances; or, at most, a psychological desire for complete impressions. So when you have told your tale, end it.

For the conclusion, as for the beginning, one paragraph is about the average length. The practice differs, of course, with different writers and different stories, but there is not so much variance as in the beginnings. An effective climax often completes a story in the most satisfactory way. In "The Ambitious Guest" Hawthorne employs three paragraphs (¶ 42-44), exclusive of the climax itself, to conclude the story. Each of these three paragraphs contains matter necessary to the completion of the tale in Hawthorne's style. It is probable that a modern writer would have condensed them into a single paragraph, because of the modern demand for extreme compression; but with the possible exception of the last two sentences of ¶ 44 there is nothing irrelevant in the conclusion. In "The Birthmark," and "Young Goodman Brown," Hawthorne uses but a single paragraph for his conclusion.

The conclusion and the climax should be as nearly simultaneous as possible. The present tendency is to make them coincide, and so increase the effect of the climax by making it the actual end of the story, as it is the end of the interest. It is not always that the coincidence can be perfect, but many a story could be cut short immediately after the climax, and be much improved thereby. For example, if Hawthorne had written "The Ambitious Guest" to-day it is probable that he would have ended it with ¶ 44: "The slide! The slide!" Had he done so he would certainly have given additional force to his climax, strong though it is now; and I believe that any reader would have understood perfectly all that is contained in ¶ 42-44. You must be careful, however, in the use of this style of conclusion, lest your supposed climax is merely an abrupt ending—a false climax—which leaves unsettled some things which a further conclusion should make clear. Not every plot allows an abrupt ending, even though it may have a good climax, and you must suit your method to your matter. In any case, the story must convey a complete impression.

But the conclusion must not be padded with irrelevant matter to make it appear rounded, or to please the perverted taste of the writer. The end is allowed scant space and has even less room for sage observations, or pointing of morals, or lamentations over the sins or misfortunes portrayed than have the other parts of the story. In the example already quoted the narrative drags on for some nine paragraphs after the story is really ended, without adding anything of interest or value. Happily such conclusions are infrequent, but the best of writers are occasionally dragged into them through their reluctance to quit forever scenes and people that have grown dear to them through close association. A somewhat similar method of padding out the conclusion to the detriment of the story is to end with a catch word referring to the beginning, as in the following example, where the "blackberry girl" is a reminder of the title:

I hope these few surprises of mine may serve as a lesson to some young man, and help to teach him to prove true to his first love, though she may appear to be only a poor girl—yes, even a "blackberry girl."

Of all poor conclusions the conventional is most to be feared by the novice, for it is surely fatal to the story to which it is attached. If the story is conventional in plot and treatment it is inevitable that its ending should be conventional, so here again we see the necessity of originality of plot. But too often a writer, after having successfully carried his story past the climax, will grow weary or careless and end it with the conventional ideas and phrases which were worn threadbare ages ago.

The inexperienced writer of the gentler sex is peculiarly liable to be guilty of using conventional endings. To her mind, apparently, the chief end of man is marriage, and the proper end of a story is a wedding. It must be acknowledged that this is the only logical conclusion to her stories, for from the moment they appear in the opening paragraphs the reader knows that in the last the hero will marry the heroine, willy nilly, at the behest of the matchmaking "authoress." "To the author, who has suffered with and on account of his characters more intensely than any reader can suffer, there is something amusing in this anxiety to have the old formula, 'And they all lived happy ever afterwards,' repeated at the end of every tale. A tiny *bonne bouche* of happiness is so inadequate after some stories of sorrow that it seems almost an irony to offer it to the readers; and yet, like children who have taken a bitter medicine, they are very likely to complain that they have had no taste of sweetness, if it is not offered to them.... The common feeling that death is inevitably sad is responsible for much of the stress which is laid upon the endings of books. That, and the belief that people who love each other can have no joy or benefit of life if they must live apart, have set up two formal and arbitrary conditions which a story must fulfil in order to be considered cheerful. The principal characters may go through fire and water if necessary, but they must get rid of their smoke stains and dry their costumes in time to appear alive and smiling in the final chapter; and the hero and the heroine must marry each other, or, if the writer has allowed their affections to wander further afield, they must at least marry the people of their choice. These, of course, are not the standards of the most thoughtful readers, and yet, like all conventionalities, they extend further than an author likes to believe."[43]

The fact is, however, that if real people were constantly thrown at one another's heads so determinedly it would take a stronger power than even the omnipotent literary aspirant to force them into matrimony. Nor are weddings, or descriptions thereof, particularly delectable reading when they desert the society column for the short story. They are usually very much alike—though one original writer did perform her ceremony up a tree—and the bride always wears the same dresses and smiles the same smiles and weeps the same tears. So if you *must* have a wedding, let the reader off with the classic formula, "And so they were married and lived happily ever after;" but don't inflict on him such cheap sentimentalism as this:

> Christmas morning was clear, cold and bright, just such a morning as had marked Fred's first departure from the Blanford's some three years before.
>
> Grace's sisters had come home to take charge of affairs for the day and evening so Grace did not have much to see after but herself. Fred, supposing he would rather be in the way, did not arrive until about an hour before the ceremony was to take place, which was in the evening. A good many guests were invited and as they had already begun to arrive, Grace but barely had time to greet Fred, when she found she must withdraw and don her wedding garment.
>
> If Grace had looked pretty with her gown held up about her a few weeks ago, she now looked handsome indeed as she came into the well crowded room.
>
> Her rich silk gown fell in deep soft folds at her dainty feet. The soft creamy lace fell about her well shaped neck in clusters; the color of the gown made her hair and eyes look black as jet; and the excitement still kept the roses in her cheeks. Fred did not look so handsome, but no one could help admire the manly form as he stood beside Grace answering the questions that were to acknowledge them man and wife.
>
> As soon as the ceremony was over and congratulations had been extended to the bride and groom, they were ushered in to a nicely prepared supper. A merry Christmas evening was spent. Grace's brothers did not lose their housekeeper, as she and Fred made their home with them.

They spent their days not like the hurrying brook, but grasped all the sunshine that was meant for them.

And in general it is much better—better art and better manners—for you to draw the reader politely aside as soon as the heroine has whispered the inevitable "Yes;" for what follows should not be spied upon by any third party.

FOOTNOTES:

[42] See "preparation for the climax" in Chapter IX.

[43] "The Problem of Endings," by Mary Tracy Earle. *The Book Buyer.* Aug. '98.

XI

THE STYLE

The method of presentation of the short story is a matter of import. Its very artificiality calls for skilled workmanship; it must be made pleasant and readable by all known devices; its brevity, too, permits and demands a higher finish than is necessary in the novel. And altogether the short story offers a writer who is not exactly a genius a rare chance to show his ability as an artist in words. Hence the question of style is of serious moment.

Style is so much a matter of individuality, and the short story comprises so broad a range of subjects, that it is not easy to lay down general rules concerning the proper style. No two masters would or could treat the same plot in precisely the same way, and yet the method of each would be correct. However, certain generalizations concerning the style of the short story may be made without being arbitrary. As always in literature, the style should be appropriate to the matter. This may seem entirely gratuitous, yet the examination of the work of amateurs will justify the remark. They are apt to treat serious subjects with the most unbecoming levity, and to dress commonplaces in an absurdly ornate style; and at times they so far disregard propriety that they offend against good taste.

The style of the short story should be simple, easy and concise. Usually the matter is not of great moment; it is incidental rather than critical; and it offers little reason for exaggerated expressions, or rotund periods. Above all it should be natural, for the short story, despite its many conventionalities, is very near to nature. The extreme sensationalism affected by many amateurs is most absurd, for nature and things true to nature can never be really sensational—a fact which is unconsciously recognized by the offending writer in his resort to artificial means to make his narrative sensational. I say "extreme sensationalism" because I believe a certain amount of what is commonly designated sensationalism is permissible in the short story to sustain the interest, and to produce that delightful "thrill" which accompanies a clever scene. The best rule for the novice is to stick close to nature—that is, to fact. He may present what startling effects he will so that he can prove them copies of nature, and so that they do not offend against art; but it is not permitted him to harrow the feelings of his readers by unduly dwelling upon exciting topics. Any undue exaggeration of this style, or any attempt to create excitement by sheer force of italics, capitals and exclamation points, is in extremely bad taste. It at once disgusts the intelligent reader, and it will soon so weary even the ignorant that he will yawn drearily over the most startling display of "scare" lines.

The necessity for a simple style must not be made an excuse for commonplaceness; and here the author confronts rather a serious question, for everyday life abounds in commonplaces, which literature will not tolerate. If we make our stories readable we must, in some degree, represent life; if we represent life we cannot wholly avoid commonplaces; if we do not avoid commonplaces we become unliterary. However, the difficulty is more easily solved than at first appears, and the solution lies in the very life which we portray. Life certainly is full of the baldest facts, but they are so subordinated to the relatively few but important events by which our lives are checkered that we shortly forget the commonplaces and remember only the striking occurrences. In like manner we should so preserve the proportion of our stories that the necessary commonplaces, while they properly perform their parts, shall be carefully subjugated to the interesting happenings. This is largely a matter of the handling, for in fiction events seem great or small in accordance with the space and treatment that they receive. The way, then, to dispose of commonplaces is to slight them as much as possible: to crowd them into the least possible space, and to couch them in ordinary language; for thoughts that are rendered unusual by their expression become conspicuous.

By ordinary language I do not mean the stereotyped phrases which the mentally lazy employ in the expression of their thoughts, but the simple, correct and rather colorless speech which is heard among the truly cultured. Indeed, sensationalism is preferable to the deadly monotony of the writer who is wont to clothe his ideas in the ready-made garments of conventional phrases; for sensationalism has at least the merit of vividness. The writer who penned the following could hardly have been more absurdly commonplace and stereotyped in his phraseology if he had been ridiculing some "popular" author of cheap literature, but he wrote in serious earnest; the story throughout is a perfect gold mine of such hackneyed expressions. I have italicized the most offensive, though it is hardly necessary.

Faint rumors of a church scandal *permeated the very atmosphere* in Frankton, and every one was *on the alert* to *catch the faintest whisper* in regard to the matter; as the minister was a *social favorite*, and it was known by *an inside few* that he was the one most seriously involved.

For a long time the matter was suppressed, and then first one hint after another leaked out that Mrs. Daniels, the minister's wife, was *a most unhappy woman*, and that there was *another woman in the case.*

At first the members of the congregation hooted at the idea; but when item after item of scandal came to their notice they begun to take a little notice, and it was noticeable that a good many enquiries were *going the rounds,* "*just to satisfy themselves* as to the ridiculous part of it", so the *curiosity seekers* explained.

Other writers attempt to make their commonplaces literary by couching them in stilted language, and then we have what is technically termed "fine writing." It is to this tendency that we owe such phrases as, "After the customary salutations he sought the arms of Morpheus," and "Upon rising in the morning he partook of an abundant repast," when the author meant merely to say, "After saying good night he went to bed," and "He breakfasted." This error is due to the mistaken idea that things which are common are necessarily vulgar, and to an absurd squeamish objection to "call a spade, a spade." It is the worst possible way to handle commonplaces, for it attracts particular attention to the very things which it is supposed to hide.

But the writer may purposely subordinate commonplace facts, and yet suffer from a commonplace style, if he fails to give his narrative character. It is then that the young writer resorts to the use of poetry, quoted and original, with which he interlards his stories and the speeches of his characters. The poetry may be good, even if it is original, and it may be very apt, but few people in real life quote poetry in their ordinary speech. You may be well read in poetry and the kindred arts, but it is hardly the part of modesty or discretion for you to force your quotations upon a reader who very likely cares neither for your erudition nor the poets themselves. It is bad technically, too; and usually, as in the case of the following specimen, shows that the author has a wider acquaintance with the poets than with the rhetoricians.

Algernon Long was not a person of unbalanced mind, nor was he superstitious in his interpretations of signs, visions and dreams to which so many attach supernatural importance; he was simply a successful man of the world, full of life and buoyancy, devoted to his occupation, that of a stock-broker, and to his domestic and social relations. And yet he believed with Lord Byron, that

"Our life is twofold; sleep hath its own world,
And a wide realm of wild reality,
And dreams that in their development have breath,
And tears and tortures and the touch of joy;
They leave a weight upon our waking thoughts,
They take a weight from off our waking toils.
They do divide our being,
They speak like sibyls of the future."

A number of his most cherished friends had recently passed away into that "undiscovered country, from whose bourne no traveller returns." The loss to him was intolerable; the experience the most painful he had ever known. Each case seemed more cruel than its predecessor; to himself personally most suggestive. He was now in mature manhood, and could thoroughly appreciate the poet's lines:

"Life is real, life is earnest,
And the grave is not its goal."

So strong is the tendency of the short story toward simplicity that even figures of speech are to be avoided. This does not mean that we are carefully to discard any expression which savors of the figurative: such a thing would be absurd, for literature and everyday speech abound in figurative language which passes current unquestioned. But figures which are introduced simply for literary effect are unnatural, and so are to be avoided. They are really digressions, excrescences—beautiful enough in themselves, perhaps, but assuredly adding no beauty to the narrative. Principal among such figures employed by amateurs are the long complex metaphors and similes in which epic poetry delights; the figure of apostrophe, too, is much affected by tyros, because it affords them opportunity to coin orotund phrases concerning the irony of fate, the haplessness of true lovers, and kindred favorite topics.

Foreign words and phrases form another sad stumbling block in the way of a simple natural style. They have their uses, of course—and one is to betray the novice. He fondly imagines that a sprinkling of French phrases gives his narrative a delightful air of cosmopolitanism; and that as an evidence of "culture" a line from Horace or Homer is equal to a college degree. So he thumbs the back of his dictionary, culls therefrom trite quotations with which to deck his writing, and never uses an English word when he knows a similar French one. The employment of a foreign word or phrase to express an idea which can be equally well couched in English is the cheapest sort of a literary trick, and it is the unmistakable badge of hopeless mediocrity and self-complacency. Expressions from other languages may be judiciously and legitimately used to give local color, and they are, of course, indispensable in the speeches of certain character types; but as a rule there is no better medium for your thoughts than good wholesome English.

You will notice that I specify the sort of English you should use, for many who avoid foreign idioms fall into the equally bad habit of using poor and incorrect English. I am not referring to the speeches of the characters, whose privileges in this respect I have already discussed; but in the necessary introductory and connective phrases you should take exquisite pains to keep your English pure. The use of slang is of course absolutely inexcusable, for it offends against good taste as well as good rhetoric; but the employment of words in a careless or perverted meaning is equally condemnable. It is also a mistake to use too many adjectives, to throw every adjective and adverb into the superlative degree, and in other ways to exaggerate every expression which you use. Much of this misuse of words is due to ignorance, but more to carelessness or laziness; in any case you can detect your faults if you seek for them, and you should take immediate steps to correct them, with the help of a dictionary, or a rhetoric, or both.

The style of the short story should be easy and flowing, so that it shall be pleasant reading. Good ideas may be expressed in good language and still be afflicted with a nervousness or stiffness of style that will make the work difficult of perusal, and so lessen its power to hold the reader. One of the first requisites for this desired ease is a lightness of phrasing which is at once a matter of thought and of rhetorical construction. Try to avoid heaviness and austerity of thought as much as you would similar qualities in writing. Get at the lighter, brighter, perhaps more frivolous side of things; do not take your work too seriously, you are seldom writing tragedies; permit yourself to be humorous, witty, a little ironical; do not plunge too deeply into dark abysses of metaphysics or theology. I do not mean that you should not treat of serious things, or that you should make light of serious subjects; but there are several ways of looking at any matter, and the atmosphere of intense and morbid gloom which Poe casts over so many of his weird tales is not characteristic of the short story in general. At the same time I am far from advocating flippancy or superficiality, for both are deadly sins in literature. I merely wish to impress upon you the absurdity of the solemn tone which some amateurs seem to think a mark of depth of thought or feeling. An apt, simple phrase is the most forceful means of expression known to literature.

Your bright thoughts should be expressed in words and sentences which are in themselves light and easy. There is a good deal of difference between words which may mean the same thing, and it is not altogether a matter of length. Words which are heavy and lumbering, or harsh, or suggestive of unpleasant thoughts, should be used with care, for their thoughtless introduction will often injure the ease of a passage. Tone color in words is of almost as much importance in prose as in verse.

Similarly the sentence structure should be carefully tested for ease. The periodic style should be practically tabooed: it is seldom appropriate to the matter of the short story, and it is always heavy and retarding. The very short sentence, which is so typical of the French, may be used only in moderation, for its excessive employment gives a nervous jerky style which is tiresome and irritating. Among American writers Stephen Crane is an awful example of this "bumpety-bump" method of expression, though his later works show a tendency to greater ease. The exclamatory and interrogative sentences, of which amateurs use so many, under the mistaken impression that they lend vivacity and vividness, should be totally eschewed. They offend against almost every principle of the short story, and they have nothing to recommend them. Usually they are irrelevant and inartistic asides by the author. The proper sentence structure for the bulk of the short story is the simple straightforward declarative sentence, rather loose, of medium length, tending to short at times to avoid monotony and give vividness.

Exclamation points must be used sparingly: a row of three or four of them at the end of a sentence is a sign of amateurism. The mere presence of a point of punctuation will not make a thrilling sentence or produce a climax. Punctuation marks are designed to draw attention to what already exists, and they have no inherent power to create interest. Very few sentences really need or merit a mark of exclamation; and if they are properly constructed the reader will feel the exclamatory force, whether the point is expressed or not. Italics, as a method of emphasis, are seldom necessary in a well-written story. They, too, are signs of what has already been expressed, and not the expression of a new force. A word or a phrase which needs sufficient emphasis to excuse italics should be so placed that the reader will involuntarily give it the proper stress; and an expression thus brought into notice far exceeds in importance one which owes its prominence to a mere change in type. Words in still more staring type—small capitals or capitals—are entirely out of place.

Finally, the style of the short story should be concise. "One of the difficulties of the short story, the short story shares with the actual drama, and that is the indispensableness of compression—the need that every sentence shall tell."[44] It is not sufficient that all irrelevant ideas be carefully pruned away; all unnecessary fullness of expression must likewise be cut, that the phrasing of the story may always be crisp and to the point. This is sometimes a matter of the expunging of a superfluous word or phrase; but it is fully as often a recasting of a sentence so as to avoid redundancy. The object of this conciseness is twofold: to waste as little as possible of the valuable and abridged space of the short story, and to make the movement of the language as quick as the action of the plot.

The fault to be avoided here is commonly called "padding." Briefly speaking the term padding, as applied to a piece of literature, denotes the presence of irrelevant matter. It may consist of the introduction of scenes, persons, episodes, conversations or general observations which have no part in advancing the action; or, more dangerous still, it may consist of the presence of occasional words and phrases which lengthen and perhaps round out the sentences without adding to their value. Irrelevant scenes, persons, episodes, conversations and general observations have already been discussed at length, and need no further treatment here. But I must warn the novice against that most insidious form of padding which is responsible for so many long and dreary sentences, cluttered with repetitious words and phrases which retard the narrative and exasperate the reader. This redundancy is a rhetorical fault, which is best corrected by a return to the old school day methods of testing a sentence for coherence. It must be corrected, and that vigorously and radically, for it is fatal to a good short story style. An instance of how much stress editors lay upon procuring only the "concentrated extract of the story-teller's art" may be found in a letter received by a young writer from the editor of a prominent publication: "We will pay $100 for your story as it is. If you can reduce it a third, we will pay you $150; if a half, $200."

Concise must not be understood to mean exhaustive, for it is bad policy to leave nothing to the imagination of the reader. The average person is fond of reading between the lines, and usually prides himself upon his ability in this respect; accordingly he is easily exasperated with the exhaustive style which leaves no chance for the exercise of his subtle power, while he takes huge delight in expanding the sly hints which the knowing writer throws out for his benefit. Such a reader never stops to consider that he has fallen into a skillfully laid trap; he compliments the author upon his artistic method and turns from the story well pleased with himself and with the writer. There is, however, something more than a pampering of pride in the charm of this suggestive method: it enables the writer to cast a light veil of uncertainty over rather bald facts, and thus to maintain that romantic glamour of unreality which plays so important a part in fiction.

A good style can be acquired by the exercise of knowledge, patience and labor. The first requisite is a practical working knowledge of rhetoric and English composition. It seems absurd to suppose that any one would attempt to write stories without being able to write correct English, but at least two-thirds of the stories submitted to editors contain inexcusable grammatical and rhetorical errors; and many of the faults which I have found it necessary to discuss in the first part of this chapter are matters of rhetoric. If you cannot write correct English now, set about perfecting yourself in that respect before you dare to essay story telling. There are books and correspondence courses galore which will assist you. If you won't do that you had better turn your energies in some other direction, for you have neither the courage nor the spirit necessary for a successful short story writer.

Your next duty is to cultivate your individuality. "Style is the personal impress which a writer inevitably sets upon his production. It is that character in what is written which results from the fact that these thoughts and emotions have been those of the author rather than of any other human being. It is the expression of one man's individuality, as sure and as unique as the sound of his voice, the look from his eye, or the imprint of his thumb."[45] Every person who has any call to write has a strong personality—an original manner of looking at life and of treating its problems. He wishes so to influence the world by this personality that it will consent to see through his eyes, or will at least listen patiently to what he sees. It is this ego, this that is the man himself, that he really desires to show through his writings. His first step, then, is to cultivate this individuality, to train his originality, so to speak, in order that he may see everything in a new and distinctive light. He should also give attention to the expression of his personality. It is not sufficient that he shall see life at a new angle, but he must so train himself that he shall be able to put in an original way the new phases which his individuality has discovered. It is this expression of the individuality which causes so much trouble, for hundreds of stories are written which show originality in conception, but which fall into conventionality in the execution. The best way to express your personality is to be perfectly natural, and say exactly what you think; any labored striving after effects will produce an artificial style which will be fatal to success.

It is a great aid to the attainment of a good style thoroughly to understand your own mind before you put pen to paper. It may seem odd that you should be ignorant of your own ideas on a subject, but often difficulty of expression is due to indecision of mind. Vagueness or confusion of ideas in a writer's mind is always the precursor of a poor style. Too often, struck by a happy thought, he attempts to put it on paper before it has yet sufficient definiteness of form to justify expression, and when he would project it into writing he loses the thought in a mass of the very words in which he seeks to voice it. Again, the writer's mind may contain several jumbled ideas, each one good in itself but totally independent of the others; and if he attempts to express any particular one before it has had time to disentangle itself, it is bound to bring with it portions of other and distinct ideas. Clear thinking is the basis of clear writing; and clear writing prevents the chief errors that threaten your style.

Study the stories of great writers; you know what parts most trouble you—compare your work with that of others and see how they have obtained the effect that you desire to produce. It is not wise to limit your study to any one writer. Your style should possess a certain flexibility, to enable it to adapt itself readily to your varying themes, and you should master the methods of all good writers; if you have sufficient individuality to have any excuse for writing you need have little fear of imitating them too closely. For style alone it is better to confine yourself to the more modern writers. There is always a change in style, if not exactly a progression, from one literary generation to the next, and you should aim at conformity to the canons of your own age. Those early masters of the short story, Irving, Hawthorne and Poe, had a tendency toward a diffuse, almost discursive style, which is not much in vogue now. Their ease and elegance are most commendable, but they lost somewhat more in force and conciseness than is thought correct to-day.

FOOTNOTES:

[44] "The Short Story," by Frederick Wedmore. *Nineteenth Century.* Mar., '98.

[45] "Talks on Writing English," by Arlo Bates. Chapter on "Style."

XII

THE LABOR OF AUTHORSHIP

BECAUSE literature is an art and you have a leaning toward it, do not therefore consider yourself a genius and so exempt from work. There is no royal road to success, and no one ever yet won a high place in the world of letters who did not earn it by the sweat of his brow. In these days literature is just as much a trade as boilermaking: it has its tools and its rules; and if one likes his occupation, he will naturally make better stories—or boilers. That is all there is to genius—the matter of aptitude for a certain thing; and even that can be to a great degree cultivated. If a man, with absolutely no knowledge of the tools and methods of the craft, attempt to make a boiler, he will create a deal of noise but no boilers, though he may be well pleased with his own efforts; and so it is with writing.

So even if your literary efforts are praised by friends and published by local editors, don't get the idea into your head that the world at large is sighing for the products of your pen: it is far more likely that your friends' encouragement is prompted rather by regard for you than by any real merit in your work, and that the editor's chief desire is to get cheap copy. You will learn later that the truest estimate of your work comes from those who know you the least, and that usually criticism is valuable in inverse proportion to the regard which the critic has for you. If, however, you feel that, whatever the real worth of your present work, there is that within you which demands utterance, you will modestly accept this early adulation as prophetic of the true fame to come, and will go about your writing in all humility and seriousness, with that careful, plodding application which alone succeeds.

Since as a story writer you purpose handling life in all its varied phases, it is necessary that you should acquire an intimate knowledge of it. This you may do in several ways, as already indicated in Chapter V., but do it you must, and seriously. You must have in your possession and ready for instant use a large and varied assortment of facts, incidents, odd characters, impressions, and all the other miscellaneous details that go to the making of a good story. However you may gain this material it is best not to depend too much on your memory to retain it and to produce it promptly at the proper time. The human memory is apt to be treacherous and unreliable. It will very likely fail to retain the important details of a usable actual occurrence, as well as the bright idea in connection with it which flashed across your mind when first you found it. The only safe way is for you to keep a scrap book and a note book, or perhaps a combination of the two, in which you may preserve crude material, bright ideas, and all sorts of odds and ends which you think may be of use to you at some future day. Much that you carefully preserve will never be of service to you, but you cannot afford to risk losing possible good matter through failure to make note of it. "I would counsel the young writer to keep a note book, and to make, as regards the use of it, *nulla dies sine linea* his revered motto. It is a great deal better that he should have his notes too copious than too meagre. By filling page after page with jottings of thoughts, fancies, impressions, even doubts and surmises of the vaguest kind—of a kind which he himself can only understand at the time and perhaps may afterward fail to recollect when re-reading them—he will never, in the long run, account himself a loser."[46]

When finally putting your ideas into concrete form do not depend too much on the "moment of inspiration." It is not my intention to ridicule this most valuable incentive to artistic work. I believe in it thoroughly when it is genuine, and I would advise you to take all advantage of it. Dash off your story as swiftly as you will—the swifter the better, for if it runs easily from your pen it stands a better chance of being spontaneous. But we are not all of us gifted with the ability to work in this manner, nor will all themes permit of such treatment. A short story that you can rush through at a sitting should be viewed with skepticism: either it is a perfect work of genius, and you have a Heaven-sent call to write; or, and more probably, it is too trite and trivial to justify the expenditure of serious labor upon it, and your "inspiration" was merely a flush of vanity. "As for trusting to the 'inspired moment,' or waiting for it, or deploring its delay, he (the young author) should take heed how he permits any such folly or superstition to clutch him in its vitiating grasp. 'Inspiration' either means, with a writer, good mental and physical health, or it has no meaning whatever.... Late hours and stimulants are especially fatal to the young writer when both are employed in the sense of literary co-adjutors."[47]

"There is, I believe, no greater fallacy than trusting to inspiration, except that of believing that a certain mood is necessary for writing. Ninety-nine hundredths of the best literary work is done by men who write to live, who know that they must write, and who do write, whether the weather is fine or rainy, whether they like their breakfast or not, whether they are hot or cold, whether they are in love, happily or unhappily, with women or themselves. Of course, a man who has lived by his pen for years, finds out by experience the hours for working which suit him best; but a beginner should be methodical. He should go to his desk as any other workman goes to his work, after breakfast; rest and eat in the middle of the day, and work again in the afternoon. He should never begin by writing at night, unless he is obliged to do so. He will, of course, often sit at the table for an hour or more without writing a word, but if he will only think conscientiously of what he meant to do, he will find the way to do it. The evening is the time to read, and the night is the time to sleep."[48]

This dependence on genius and inspiration is one of the reasons why the world is so full of unliterary writers, and why so many of real talent fail of success. It is very easy, in the flush of composition, to consider yourself gifted above your fellows, and to go on writing reams of bosh that even you would despise, if you could view it with an unprejudiced eye; and it is equally easy to persuade yourself that anything that comes from your pen must be incapable of improvement, and that if your writings sell, you have reached the goal. But either delusion is fatal. In short, "inspiration" and all its attendant follies are but the conventional accompaniments of literary toil, which may be affected by the *dilettante* for the furthering of his pretense at art, but which have no place in the thoughts or plans of the serious worker.

Such inspiration as you may need to keep your work fresh and artistic will come to you from the zeal and interest with which you approach your task. If you go to it half-heartedly, lazy in body and mind, and ready at the first opportunity to put it all off till the morrow, you will accomplish little, then or ever; but if, on the contrary, you will square yourself to your writing as to a physical labor, and will concentrate all the powers and energies of your mind upon the work in hand, the very force of your will and your desire will create within you an enthusiasm which will be of far more practical value to you than any cheap inspiration drawn from some Parnassian spring. You can, in fact, by this very business-like method of working, create on demand a species of inspiration, or mental vigor, which will enable you, not exactly to dash off a masterpiece with no real effort on your part, but to achieve by actual labor those things which you desire to do. There is much, too, in going to your work regularly, even as a carpenter to his bench; for the mental processes that produce good short stories are capable of cultivation and control; and, like all functions of the brain, they approach the nearest to perfection when they fall into something of a routine of habit. Indeed, they may be so far regulated that at the usual hour for their exercise they will be not only active but urgent, so that you will go to your work with an appetite as hearty as that with which you welcome the dinner hour.

Do not be afraid of the manual labor of authorship—the writing and rewriting, the testing and correcting, the persistent and thorough "licking into shape" which gives the final polish to your work. Never send an editor a penciled, smutched, and disorderly MS., with a note saying, "I just dashed this off last night and send it right on." Such work is foredoomed to failure. But when your story is finished lay it away without even reading it over and let it get "cold;" leave it for a week, or two weeks, or even longer if possible—don't even think of it; then bring it forth and read it over carefully and critically, take your blue pencil, harden your heart, and rework it ruthlessly. In the first draft you are bound to slight certain places or to make certain errors, which you would correct in the course of a careful revision. There will be some half-formed thought which will need elaboration, or some word which was not quite the right one, but which you let pass lest you lose your train of thought; and there is almost sure to be some wordiness which will need cutting away.

"For, if the practice of composition be useful, the laborious work of correcting is no less so: it is indeed absolutely necessary to our reaping any benefit from the habit of composition. What we have written should be laid by for some little time, till the ardor of composition be past, till the fondness for the expressions we have used be worn off, and the expressions themselves be forgotten; and then reviewing our work with a cool and critical eye, as if it were the performance of another, we shall discern many imperfections which at first escaped us. Then is the right season for pruning redundances; for weighing the arrangement of sentences; for attending to the junctures and connecting particles; and bringing style into a regular, correct, and supported form. This '*Limae Labor*' must be submitted to by all who communicate their thoughts with proper advantage to others; and some practice in it will soon sharpen their eye to the most necessary objects of attention, and render it a much more easy and practicable work than might at first be imagined."[49]

It is this last careful, minute testing and polishing which will determine whether or no you are serious in your endeavor to break into literature, for here the real labor of authorship begins. All that went before was simply child's play compared to this grubbing, plodding, tinkering, and patching, and pottering; so if you have no stomach for this, you had better learn a trade. "Whatever you do, take pains with it. Try at least to write good English: learn to criticise and correct your work: put your best into every sentence. If you are too lazy and careless to do that, better go into a trade or politics: it is easier to become a Congressman or millionaire than a real author, and we have too many bad story-tellers as it is."[50] If you will pursue this labor of revision courageously you will speedily find an improvement in the quality of your finished work. You will also find that your manuscripts need less after attention, for the lessons learned in these careful re-workings will be unconsciously applied during composition.

"From the alphabetic slovenliness which will not form its letters legibly nor put in its commas, to the lack of self-acquaintance which results in total disability to judge one's own products, it is too constantly in evidence that those who aspire to feed other minds are themselves in need of discipline.... It is within bounds to say that not one accepted manuscript out of ten is fit to go to the printer as it stands."[51] Do not be so lazy or so careless as to slight the little things, the mere mechanical details, which go to make a perfect story and a presentable manuscript. "There are several distinct classes of errors to look for: faults of grammar, such as the mixing of figures of speech. Faults of agreement of verbs and participles in number when collective nouns are referred to. Faults of rhetoric, such as the mixing of moods and tenses, and the taste, such as the use of words with a disagreeable or misleading atmosphere about them, though their strict meaning makes their use correct enough. Faults of repetition of the same word in differing senses in the same sentence or paragraph. Faults of tediousness of phrasing or explanation. Faults of lack of clearness in expressing the exact meaning. Faults of sentimental use of language, that is, falling into fine phrases which have no distinct meaning—the most discordant fault of all. Faults of digression in the structure of the story."[52]

Faults in grammar and rhetoric are too easily corrected to be allowed to stand in the way of your success, and I have already showed you how you may perfect yourself in these essentials. For they are essentials, and so much more important than many young writers think, that I believe I am perfectly safe in saying that no one who makes glaring rhetorical or grammatical errors has ever written a successful short story. In spelling, too, there is absolutely no excuse for errors; you surely know if you are weak in this respect, and the use of even a small dictionary will enable you to avoid mistakes. Every magazine has its own rules for punctuation and paragraphing, in accordance with which an accepted MS. is edited before it is given to the compositor; but that is no good reason why you should neglect to prepare your MS. properly. The general rules are few and easily understood, and they enable you to give your work definite form and arrangement, and make it much more easy to read. An editor who finds a MS. lacking in these lesser essentials will be apt to throw it aside with but a superficial perusal, naturally judging that it will also lack the higher attributes.

Finally, just before sending your story out for editorial consideration, go over it once more with the utmost care and painstakingly test every paragraph, every sentence, every word, to see first if it is necessary, and second if it is right. If at any point you find yourself questioning what you have written, do not call your work complete until you have revised it, not only to your own satisfaction, but so that you honestly feel that the reader, too, will be satisfied. If you cannot at the time arrive at a satisfactory expression of your thought, put the story aside for the time being and try again later when you can come to it afresh. It is this unwearied labor which in the end spells success.

FOOTNOTES:

[46] "Some Advice to Young Authors," by Edward Fawcett. *The Independent.* May 14, '96.

[47] "Some Advice to Young Authors," by Edgar Fawcett. *The Independent.* May 14, '96.

[48] "The Art of Authorship." Edited by George Bainton. Chapter by F. Marion Crawford.

[49] "Lectures on Rhetoric and Belles Letters," by Hugh Blair. Lecture XIX.

[50] "Bad Story-Telling," by Frederick M. Bird. *Lippincott's.* Oct., '97.

[51] *Ibid.*

[52] "How to Write Fiction." Anonymous. Bellaires & Co., London. Part II. Chapter IV.

XIII

THE QUEST OF A MARKET

EVEN when his story is complete the writer has not yet come to the end of his difficulties, for he has still to find a market for his work. Since he is writing for publication, and not for the mere love of composition, this quest of a market is an important matter, for by his success in this respect the writer must judge his chances of ultimate and material success as a short story writer. There is no disputing the fact that good work will find acceptance eventually, but sometimes the delay is so long that the writer almost loses hope. He usually goes about marketing his wares in a haphazard fashion; and a warning word or two at this point may enable him to remedy some of the mistakes which may retard if not prevent the success of really meritorious work.

In the first place, then, consider your story honestly and without prejudice, and make sure that it does deserve publication. Get an unbiased opinion on it from some real critic, if you can, and give some weight to what he says. Never, like many novices I have known, send out a MS. with an accompanying note saying that you know your story is not quite up to standard, and that you could improve it if you had the time, but that you hope the editor will make an exception in your favor in order to encourage you. Editors are not paid to do that sort of thing; and if you yourself have not complete confidence in your story you have no business to inflict it upon an editor. If you enter the profession of story writing in that spirit you will fail, absolutely and deservedly, to gain aught but rebuffs by your labors; and indeed, your labor will be so slight and half hearted that you cannot honestly expect any satisfactory return from it.

Emerson's advice, "Hitch your wagon to a star," is an excellent rule for the young writer. With you literature may be a profession as well as an art, but you should not permit yourself to be too easily satisfied with material success. Do not be content just because you get your work published, or because you are sure you write as well as some of your contemporaries; always try to rise above the crowd and to be one of the few who set the standard for the multitude. If your stories are accepted by one magazine, try to "break into" another that is a little more particular; if you succeed in one style of literature, try to win laurels in a higher class of work. It is this constant striving that brings ultimate success—financial and artistic. If you allow yourself to be easily content with your work and your receipts therefrom, you will speedily fall into a rut, become "old fogy" and dull, and one day will find yourself with a desk full of rejected MSS., and no hope for a brighter future.

At the same time, there are almost as many grades of stories as there are publications using them, and with but few exceptions you may endeavor to satisfy all tastes. A story which is too slight for a high class magazine may be well adapted to the needs of a newspaper syndicate; and though it would be fatal for you to take the newspaper story for your standard, there can be no objection to your making occasional contributions to that class of literature. Indeed, it is probable that at the outset you will be forced to content yourself with writing for syndicates and minor magazines, though you may aim for the pages of the best monthlies: those old established publications are both conservative and overstocked, and though they are ready enough to examine MSS., they are slow to accept the work of a young writer. But even among the few magazines which can be called first class there are wide differences of opinion as to what constitutes a good story, and a MS. which one will reject decidedly another may accept gladly. It is your first business to acquaint yourself with the general style of the magazine to which you desire to contribute; or, if your story is already written, to make sure that its acceptance is not forbidden by the policy of the publication to which you submit it. It is a waste of time and postage to send a story of adventure to a magazine which publishes only tales of love.

The timeliness, or seasonal appropriateness, of a story may have much influence upon its success in the market. Each season of the year has its peculiar literature, and editors in general place so much stress upon timeliness that a glance at the contents of a magazine will often tell you within a month of its date of issue. There are the blizzard stories, which are due about January; and the vacation stories, which begin to appear in July, and the stories of holly and mistletoe and stockings, which come with the Christmas season. Likewise, we have special stories for New Years', St. Valentine's Day, Washington's Birthday, Easter, May Day, Memorial Day, Fourth of July, Thanksgiving, and a host of minor special occasions. The plot and matter for these stories of occasions are so trite and conventional that it is a wonder that the reading public did not rebel against them long ago; but there is a constant demand for such stories, and the writer who can give the old plots some freshness is sure of a good market. Such stories should always be submitted at least three months before they are to be used, for special editions are compiled far in advance; but a story of this character is always a marketable commodity and may be carried over from year to year without deterioration.

Of a more ephemeral type are the stories whose timeliness depends upon their coinciding with the current fashion in short stories. For there are fashions in literature just as surely as in matters of dress, and short stories are peculiarly subject to such changes. A few years ago dialect was all the cry, and a story was judged and valued according to the amount of unintelligible gibberish that it contained; before that romantic adventure was most in demand; and still earlier it was bald realism; at the time of writing (Spring of 1900) war stories hold first place in popular esteem. The reason for the present style is obvious, but in general these modes are difficult to explain and almost impossible to forecast. Such stories contain no new plot, and for their timeliness depend entirely upon the introduction of the current fashion, whatever it may be; but they afford a grateful variety to the rather monotonous run of light fiction. They also offer the up-to-date writer unusual opportunities to gain editorial favor, for a story observant of the current mode is sure of serious consideration.

You should make it a rule from the start never to give away a story for the mere sake of seeing your name in print. What is worth writing and publishing is worth being paid for. Don't let a publisher persuade you that the appearance of your work in his journal will bring you a fame and a name that will enable you to sell MSS. elsewhere. Every editor knows how such a man gets his matter, and values his contributors accordingly; and every publication which can assist you in your career pays for whatever matter it uses. Besides, by giving away your stories you injure the literary market, both for yourself and for your fellow workers. If all writers resolutely declined to part with their work except for a cash equivalent, those scheming editors would soon be brought to time and forced to pay for matter to fill their columns.

Spare no pains to make your MSS. neat and legible. The fact that you are as yet little known is undoubtedly against you; your mere name has no power to exact a careful perusal of your story, and a judgment in accordance with its merits; so it is your business to gain that favor by making it easy for the editor. The question of legibility sums up the whole tale. The average editor always has his desk piled high with unsolicited MSS. from unknown writers which he must worry through after a fashion, lest something really good should escape him. He is conscientious enough, but he is always overworked, and he has learned by experience to judge a MS. almost at a glance. If he reads beyond the first page of your story, it is good evidence that he found there something of merit, even though he finally reject it. A penciled MS., or one that is written on both sides of the paper, will hardly get a passing glance. Even a neat pen-written MS. will fare little better, for to the editor a typewritten story means not only easy reading but probably some experience on the part of the author. Have your story typewritten, then, by some one who can put it in presentable shape, so that it will look business like. For mailing it is best to fold it as little as possible; the large legal envelope, requiring two folds, is most used. Unless the MS. is bulky or is on unusually small sheets, it is best to fold it at least once, for if sent flat it usually arrives in a crumpled state. Never roll it, under any circumstances, for a MS. once rolled can never be smoothed out, and no editor will bother with it.

Make the letter accompanying your story as short and business like as possible. Don't tell the editor your family history or relate how you came to write the story; don't ask him for criticisms or suggestions; say that you submit such a MS. subject to his approval, and give your name and address. That is all he cares to know about you. Always enclose stamps for return of MS.—or, better yet, a stamped and self-addressed envelope; never be so small or so careless as to underpay the postage.

It is of course your privilege to put a price upon any matter that you may submit for publication; but unless the magazine editorially requests a set price I should advise you to leave that matter to the editor, and to submit your work "at the usual rates." It is a peculiarity of the literary business that usually the buyer rather than the seller makes the terms, and until your name has a value you are hardly in position to run counter to custom. Nor is it likely that you have had sufficient experience to enable you to estimate your work justly. You need have no fear of being cheated, for a reputable publishing house is always willing to pay a fit price for suitable MSS.

It will do you no good to get a letter from some well known author or public person recommending your work to the publisher; and it will often do harm. Matter from novices is accepted on its merits alone, and no amount of praise from a man of letters or an influential friend will make your story one whit better than it was when you gave it the finishing touches. The most such intercession can accomplish is a perusal of your MS., and that you can yourself obtain if you will make it presentable. If you imagine that an editor will be influenced in his judgment by the words of an outsider, you are sadly mistaken—he is far more apt to be prejudiced against you. He is an experienced and competent man, who knows exactly what he wants, and who may naturally be expected to resent any such impertinent interference with his work.

It seems a small thing for you to ask an editor to give you a criticism on your work, and many a young writer has long cherished a grudge against some editor who has totally ignored his urgent and flattering request for a candid opinion. There is no question that even a word from an editor would be of untold value to the novice; but the novice has no idea what his request means. Every magazine is at great expense for the employment of trained "readers" to pass upon the unsolicited MSS. submitted to it, and the according of even a word of criticism to each would at least double that expense. Then, too, three-fourths of the MSS. submitted to any editor are such that he could not honestly say anything good of them, and no editor cares to go out of his way to hurt the feelings of the writer; nor would it be policy for him to do so. Every time you submit a MS. to an editor you are in a manner imposing on him, so be as easy on him as possible. If you feel that you must have an expert opinion on your work, send it to one of the literary bureaus which have been established for just that purpose. They will give you a careful and just criticism for the payment of a nominal fee.

Do not rest your hopes of success upon the fate of one MS. If you never write a new story until its predecessor has been placed you cannot possibly live long enough to win success. You should be constantly turning out new stories, each one better than the last; or reworking an old one whose faults you have just discovered; and you should keep the mails loaded with your work. You can never have too many good stories on the road.

Do not become impatient if you do not receive a check for your story within a week after sending it out. The largest magazines usually require three months and sometimes longer to report on a MS. If you attempt to hurry the editorial decision you will probably receive your MS. by return mail, unread.

It is advisable that you keep a MS. memorandum book of some sort, in which you may record the journeyings of your MSS., so that you may know where they have been and how long they have been away. You do not want to send the same MS. to the same editor twice, nor to continue submitting matter to a magazine which is already overstocked, or which is careless in returning your work. If you trust to your memory, or to some slip shod method, you will regret it in the end, for you will not only lose many MSS., but you will be submitting your work in a hit-or-miss fashion that is little likely to get it into the proper hands. There are several books of this sort on the market, or you can easily make one for yourself from an ordinary blank book. It may take any form you please, but I would suggest that it should include spaces for the number of words in the story and the postage required to carry it, besides the publishers to whom it is submitted and the dates when it is mailed and returned.

The rejection of your MS. by one or two editors should not discourage you: you may try twelve editors and have the thirteenth accept it. It is seldom indeed that it finds place where it is first submitted: it may not just meet the ideals of that editor; or he may already have too much matter on hand. If you believe the story is good, keep it going till it has been the rounds: you may find that the dawn of success comes from the point whence you least expected it.

APPENDIX

"THE AMBITIOUS GUEST"

(From Nathaniel Hawthorne's "Twice-Told Tales.")

I. One September night a family had gathered round their hearth and piled it high with the driftwood of mountain-streams, the dry cones of the pine, and the splintered ruins of great trees that had come crashing down the precipice. Up the chimney roared the fire, and brightened the room with its broad blaze. The faces of the father and mother had a sober gladness; the children laughed. The eldest daughter was the image of Happiness at seventeen, and the aged grandmother, who sat knitting in the warmest place, was the image of Happiness grown old. They had found the "herb heart's-ease" in the bleakest spot of all New England. This family were situated in the Notch of the White Hills, where the wind was sharp throughout the year and pitilessly cold in the winter, giving their cottage all its fresh inclemency before it descended on the valley of the Saco. They dwelt in a cold spot and a dangerous one, for a mountain towered above their heads so steep that the stones would often rumble down its sides and startle them at midnight.

2. The daughter had just uttered some simple jest that filled them all with mirth, when the wind came through the Notch and seemed to pause before their cottage, rattling the door with a sound of wailing and lamentation before it passed into the valley. For a moment it saddened them, though there was nothing

unusual in the tones. But the family were glad again when they perceived that the latch was lifted by some traveler whose footsteps had been unheard amid the dreary blast which heralded his approach and waited as he was entering and went moaning away from the door.

3. Though they dwelt in such a solitude, these people held daily converse with the world. The romantic pass of the Notch is a great artery through which the life-blood of internal commerce is continually throbbing between Maine on the one side and the Green Mountains and the shores of the St. Lawrence on the other. The stage-coach always drew up before the door of the cottage. The wayfarer with no companion but his staff paused here to exchange a word, that the sense of loneliness might not utterly overcome him ere he could pass through the cleft of the mountain or reach the first house in the valley. And here the teamster on his way to Portland market would put up for the night, and, if a bachelor, might sit an hour beyond the usual bedtime and steal a kiss from the mountain-maid at parting. It was one of those primitive taverns where the traveler pays only for food and lodging, but meets with a homely kindness beyond all price. When the footsteps were heard, therefore, between the outer door and the inner one, the whole family rose up, grandmother, children and all, as if about to welcome some one who belonged to them, and whose fate was linked with theirs.

4. The door was opened by a young man. His face at first wore the melancholy expression, almost despondency, of one who travels a wild and bleak road at nightfall and alone, but soon brightened up when he saw the kindly warmth of his reception. He felt his heart spring forward to meet them all, from the old woman who wiped a chair with her apron to the little child that held out its arms to him. One glance and smile placed the stranger on a footing of innocent familiarity with the eldest daughter.

5. "Ah! this fire is the right thing," cried he, "especially when there is such a pleasant circle round it. I am quite benumbed, for the Notch is just like the pipe of a great pair of bellows; it has blown a terrible blast in my face all the way from Bartlett."

6. "Then you are going toward Vermont?" said the master of the house as he helped to take a light knapsack off the young man's shoulders.

7. "Yes, to Burlington, and far enough beyond," replied he. "I meant to have been at Ethan Crawford's to-night but a pedestrian lingers along such a road as this. It is no matter; for when I saw this good fire and all your cheerful faces, I felt as if you had kindled it on purpose for me and were waiting my arrival. So I shall sit down among you and make myself at home."

8. The frank-hearted stranger had just drawn his chair up to the fire when something like a heavy footstep was heard without rushing down the steep side of the mountain as with long and rapid strides, and taking such a leap in passing the cottage as to strike the opposite precipice. The family held their breath, because they knew the sound, and their guest held his by instinct.

9. "The old mountain has thrown a stone at us for fear we should forget him," said the landlord, recovering himself. "He sometimes nods his head and threatens to come down, but we are old neighbors, and agree together pretty well, upon the whole. Besides, we have a sure place of refuge hard by if he should be coming in good earnest."

10. Let us now suppose the stranger to have finished his supper of bear's meat, and by his natural felicity of manner to have placed himself on a footing of kindness with the whole family; so that they talked together as freely as if he belonged to their mountain-brood. He was of a proud yet gentle spirit, haughty and reserved among the rich and great, but ever ready to stoop his head to the lowly cottage door and be like a brother or a son at the poor man's fireside. In the household of the Notch he

found warmth and simplicity of feeling, the pervading intelligence of New England, and a poetry of native growth which they had gathered when they very little thought of it from the mountain-peaks and chasms, and at the very threshold of their romantic and dangerous abode. He had traveled far and alone; his whole life, indeed, had been a solitary path, for, with the lofty caution of his nature, he had kept himself apart from those who might otherwise have been his companions. The family, too, though so kind and hospitable, had that consciousness of unity among themselves and separation from the world at large which in every domestic circle should still keep a holy place where no stranger may intrude. But this evening a prophetic sympathy impelled the refined and educated youth to pour out his heart before the simple mountaineers, and constrained them to answer him with the same free confidence. And thus it should have been. Is not the kindred of a common fate a closer tie than that of birth?

11. The secret of the young man's character was a high and abstracted ambition. He could have borne to live an undistinguished life, but not to be forgotten in the grave. Yearning desire had been transformed to hope, and hope, long cherished, had become like certainty that, obscurely as he journeyed now, a glory was to beam on all his pathway, though not, perhaps, while he was treading it. But when posterity should gaze back into the gloom of what was now the present, they would trace the brightness of his footsteps, brightening as meaner glories faded, and confess that a gifted one had passed from his cradle to his tomb with none to recognize him.

12. "As yet," cried the stranger, his cheek glowing and his eye flashing with enthusiasm—"as yet I have done nothing. Were I to vanish from the earth to-morrow, none would know so much of me as you—that a nameless youth came up at nightfall from the valley of the Saco, and opened his heart to you in the evening, and passed through the Notch by sunrise, and was seen no more. Not a soul would ask, 'Who was he? Whither did the wanderer

go?' But I cannot die till I have achieved my destiny. Then let Death come: I shall have built my monument."

13. There was a continual flow of natural emotion gushing forth amid abstracted reverie which enabled the family to understand this young man's sentiments, though so foreign from their own. With quick sensibility of the ludicrous, he blushed at the ardor into which he had been betrayed.

14. "You laugh at me," said he, taking the eldest daughter's hand and laughing at himself. "You think my ambition as nonsensical as if I were to freeze myself to death on the top of Mount Washington only that people might spy at me from the country roundabout. And truly that would be a noble pedestal for a man's statue."

15. "It is better to sit here by this fire," answered the girl, blushing, "and be comfortable and contented, though nobody thinks about us."

16. "I suppose," said her father, after a fit of musing, "there is something natural in what the young man says; and if my mind had been turned that way, I might have felt just the same.—It is strange, wife, how his talk has set my head running on things that are pretty certain never to come to pass."

17. "Perhaps they may," observed the wife. "Is the man thinking what he will do when he is a widower?"

18. "No, no!" cried he, repelling the idea with reproachful kindness. "When I think of your death, Esther, I think of mine too. But I was wishing we had a good farm in Bartlett or Bethlehem or Littleton, or some other township round the White Mountains, but not where they could tumble on our heads. I should want to stand well with my neighbors and be called squire and sent to General Court for a term or two; for a plain, honest man may do as much good there as a lawyer. And when I should be grown quite an old man, and you an old woman, so as

not to be long apart, I might die happy enough in my bed, and leave you all crying around me. A slate gravestone would suit me as well as a marble one, with just my name and age, and a verse of a hymn, and something to let people know that I lived an honest man and died a Christian."

19. "There, now!" exclaimed the stranger; "it is our nature to desire a monument, be it slate or marble, or a pillar of granite, or a glorious memory in the universal heart of man."

20. "We're in a strange way to-night," said the wife, with tears in her eyes. "They say it's a sign of something when folk's minds go a-wandering so. Hark to the children!"

21. They listened accordingly. The younger children had been put to bed in another room, but with an open door between; so that they could be heard talking busily among themselves. One and all seemed to have caught the infection from the fireside circle, and were outvying each other in wild wishes and childish projects of what they would do when they came to be men and women. At length a little boy, instead of addressing his brothers and sisters, called out to his mother.

22. "I'll tell you what I wish, mother," cried he: "I want you and father and grandma'm, and all of us, and the stranger too, to start right away and go and take a drink out of the basin of the Flume."

23. Nobody could help laughing at the child's notion of leaving a warm bed and dragging them from a cheerful fire to visit the basin of the Flume—a brook which tumbles over the precipice deep within the Notch.

24. The boy had hardly spoken, when a wagon rattled along the road and stopped a moment before the door. It appeared to contain two or three men who were cheering their hearts with the rough chorus of a song which resounded in broken notes

between the cliffs, while the singers hesitated whether to continue their journey or put up here for the night.

25. "Father," said the girl, "they are calling you by name."

26. But the good man doubted whether they had really called him, and was unwilling to show himself too solicitous of gain by inviting people to patronize his house. He therefore did not hurry to the door, and, the lash being soon applied, the travelers plunged into the Notch, still singing and laughing, though their music and mirth came back drearily from the heart of the mountain.

27. "There, mother!" cried the boy, again; "they'd have given us a ride to the Flume."

28. Again they laughed at the child's pertinacious fancy for a night-ramble. But it happened that a light cloud passed over the daughter's spirit; she looked gravely into the fire and drew a breath that was almost a sigh. It forced its way, in spite of a little struggle to repress it. Then, starting and blushing, she looked quickly around the circle, as if they had caught a glimpse into her bosom. The stranger asked what she had been thinking of.

29. "Nothing," answered she, with a downcast smile; "only I felt lonesome just then."

30. "Oh, I have always had a gift of feeling what is in other people's hearts," said he, half seriously. "Shall I tell the secret of yours? For I know what to think when a young girl shivers by a warm hearth and complains of lonesomeness at her mother's side. Shall I put these feelings into words?"

31. "They would not be a girl's feelings any longer if they could be put into words," replied the mountain-nymph, laughing, but avoiding his eye.

32. All this was said apart. Perhaps a germ of love was springing in their hearts so pure that it might blossom in Paradise, since it could not be matured on earth; for women worship such gentle dignity as his, and the proud, contemplative, yet kindly, soul is oftenest captivated by simplicity like hers. But while they spoke softly, and he was watching the happy sadness, the lightsome shadows, the shy yearnings, of a maiden's nature, the wind through the Notch took a deeper and drearier sound. It seemed, as the fanciful stranger said, like the choral strain of the spirits of the blast who in old Indian times had their dwelling among these mountains and made their heights and recesses a sacred region. There was a wail along the road as if a funeral were passing. To chase away the gloom, the family threw pine-branches on their fire till the dry leaves crackled and the flame arose, discovering once again a scene of peace and humble happiness. The light hovered about them fondly and caressed them all. There were the little faces of the children peeping from their bed apart, and here the father's frame of strength, the mother's subdued and careful mien, the high-browed youth, the budding girl, and the good old grandma, still knitting in the warmest place.

33. The aged woman looked up from her task, and with fingers ever busy was the next to speak.

34. "Old folks have their notions," said she, "as well as young ones. You've been wishing and planning and letting your heads run on one thing and another till you've set my mind a-wandering too. Now, what should an old woman wish for, when she can go but a step or two before she comes to her grave? Children, it will haunt me night and day till I tell you."

35. "What is it, mother?" cried the husband and wife at once.

36. Then the old woman, with an air of mystery which drew the circle closer round the fire, informed them that she had provided her grave-clothes some years before—a nice linen shroud, a cap with a muslin ruff, and everything of a finer sort

than she had worn since her wedding day. But this evening an old superstition had strangely recurred to her. It used to be said in her younger days that if anything were amiss with a corpse—if only the ruff were not smooth or the cap did not set right—the corpse, in the coffin and beneath the clods, would strive to put up its cold hands and arrange it. The bare thought made her nervous.

37. "Don't talk so, grandmother," said the girl, shuddering.

38. "Now," continued the old woman, with singular earnestness, yet smiling strangely at her own folly, "I want one of you, my children, when your mother is dressed and in the coffin,—I want one of you to hold a looking-glass over my face. Who knows but I may take a glimpse at myself and see whether all's right?"

39. "Old and young, we dream of graves and monuments," murmured the stranger youth. "I wonder how mariners feel when the ship is sinking and they, unknown and undistinguished, are to be buried together in the ocean, that wide and nameless sepulcher?"

40. For a moment the old woman's ghastly conception so engrossed the minds of her hearers that a sound abroad in the night, rising like the roar of a blast, had grown broad, deep and terrible before the fated group were conscious of it. The house and all within it trembled; the foundations of the earth seemed to be shaken, as if this awful sound were the peal of the last trump. Young and old exchanged one wild glance and remained an instant pale, affrighted, without utterance or power to move. Then the same shriek burst simultaneously from all their lips:

41. "The slide! The slide!"

42. The simplest words must intimate, but not portray, the unutterable horror of the catastrophe. The victims rushed from their cottage and sought refuge in what they deemed a safer spot,

where, in contemplation of such an emergency, a sort of barrier had been reared. Alas! they had quitted their security and fled right into the pathway of destruction. Down came the whole side of the mountain in a cataract of ruin. Just before it reached the house the stream broke into two branches, shivered not a window there, but overwhelmed the whole vicinity, blocked up the road and annihilated everything in its dreadful course. Long ere the thunder of that great slide had ceased to roar among the mountains the mortal agony had been endured and the victims were at peace. Their bodies were never found.

43. The next morning the light smoke was seen stealing from the cottage chimney up the mountainside. Within, the fire was yet smouldering on the hearth, and the chairs in a circle round it, as if the inhabitants had but gone forth to view the devastation of the slide and would shortly return to thank Heaven for their miraculous escape. All had left separate tokens by which those who had known the family were made to shed a tear for each. Who has not heard their name? The story has been told far and wide, and will forever be a legend of these mountains. Poets have sung their fate.

44. There were circumstances which led some to suppose that a stranger had been received into the cottage on this awful night, and had shared the catastrophe of all its inmates; others denied that there were sufficient grounds for such a conjecture. Woe for the high-souled youth with his dream of earthly immortality! His name and person utterly unknown, his history, his way of life, his plans, a mystery never to be solved, his death and his existence equally a doubt,—whose was the agony of that death moment?

THE END

www.ingramcontent.com/pod-product-compliance
Lightning Source LLC
Chambersburg PA
CBHW081618100526
44590CB00021B/3499